PREPARE TO DIE

PREPARE TO DIE

Living with Purpose, Dying in Peace

Mark Bellows M.Div., LMFT

XULON PRESS

Xulon Press
2301 Lucien Way #415
Maitland, FL 32751
407.339.4217
www.xulonpress.com

Paperback ISBN-13: 978-1-66281-845-5
Ebook ISBN-13: 978-1-66281-846-2

To

Jersa, Gabriel, Josiah, Joelle, Jedaiah, and Noel

And to

Layla, Paisley, and Josie.

Just writing your names brings joy to my heart.

This book contains what I believe with
all my heart.

Table of Contents

Acknowledgments ix

Introduction xi

1:   Facts, Faces, and Fears. 1

2:   Peaceful Sleep. 17

3:   No Hope, False Hope, or Living Hope. 33

4:   Numbering Our Days 49

5:   Leaving a Lasting Legacy 63

6:   The Power of "I am" 79

7:   Facing the Final Curtain 93

8:   Finishing Well. 107

9:   Going Home. 121

10: Touring Heaven 137

11: I Can't Leave you with a Bad Goodbye. . . . 153

12: Last Words. 169

13: This Changes Everything 185

Acknowledgments

My heartfelt gratitude to:

Robert Bellows for proofreading, editing, and saving me from butchering the King's English.

Jennifer Chalfy for assisting this computer-challenged caveman.

Mary Stevens for the photo on the cover in which she is holding the hand of her 100-year-old grandfather, Pete Rieken.

My Hope Community Church family for their encouragement as they endured my teaching through this material.

The patient and professional staff at Xulon Press for their guidance through this journey.

Introduction

The book you hold in your hands emerged from the trenches of the front lines of personal experience. I have officiated at over 900 funerals in my career as a pastor, I have been on scene at over 500 death occurrences as a police chaplain, and I have listened for hours and hours to unrelenting grief stories as a therapist.

Having worked for years in close proximity to death, I am fully aware that we live every moment on the brink. At every moment we could be just a heartbeat away from death. Yet so few are prepared to die and so few possess a peace about dying.

There is a line in a funeral prayer in the United Methodist *Book of Worship* that reads: "Help us to live as those who are prepared to die." This book is about helping people live. It is about living purposefully and passionately, but I would contend that one cannot embrace life fully unless one is prepared to die.

When we speak of being prepared for death, we generally think of getting our affairs in order—wills and medical directives and funeral plans. But there is a preliminary and more primary issue that will be addressed in this book. To die in peace, one must have steadfast conviction and hope-filled confidence in what lies beyond death's door.

It is troubling that so few Christians possess the ability to present a biblically grounded belief system about death and the afterlife. Too many have built a house upon the sands of empty philosophies and sentimentalism, which provide little solace or serenity at death. This book is, therefore, unapologetically based on Scriptural truths that provide purpose for living and peace in dying. It is by no means a scholarly tome. It does, however, contain information that few are able to articulate.

I hope you find the pages that follow comforting, inspiring, thought provoking, and occasionally humorous. I hope most of all that you will come to know Jesus more deeply and intimately.

Chapter 1

Facts, Faces, and Fears

L et me introduce you to a woman named Jeanne Louise Calment (Zan lwiz kalmã). Let's call her Jenny. Jenny holds the distinction of being the oldest human being whose age has been authenticated by modern standards. She was born in the year 1875 and died in 1997 at the age of 122 years and 164 days. That is a lot of birthday candles! Her longevity attracted media attention and medical curiosity in regard to her health and lifestyle secrets.

An interesting side story about Jenny—at age 90 she signed a contract on her residence, selling the property in exchange for the right of continued occupancy and a monthly payment of 2,500 francs until her death. As an investment opportunity, would you have offered that proposal?

Hmm, an expenditure of approximately 450 dollars a month until this 90-year-old woman dies in exchange for her residence. That sounds like a sure bet, a great return on investment. I would propose that business deal. But Jenny continued to live for an additional 32 years, 20 of those years in that residence. She later commented on that situation by saying, "In life, one sometimes makes bad deals."

So what were the reasons for Jenny's longevity? Surprisingly, Jenny spent her life doing many things that doctors advise against. She smoked cigarettes and an occasional cigar from age 21 until she quit at age 117, she drank cheap port wine, she polished off meals with a dessert, she often ate two pounds of chocolate a week, and she never ate breakfast. Jenny ascribed her longevity and relatively youthful appearance to eating a diet rich in olive oil, to laughing a lot, and to not getting stressed out. There is a lot we could learn from that smart old bird.

When a reporter asked Jenny what she liked best about being so old, she quipped wryly, "Well, there's no peer pressure." On her 120th birthday it is claimed that she said, "I only have one wrinkle, and I'm sitting on it." (I saw that on the Internet, it must be true.)

The Fact of Death

In contrast to Jenny, the average life span for a male in this country is currently 76.6 years and the "weaker" sex's average life expectancy is 81.1 years (2016, National Vital Statistics System). I will give you a moment to do your own math. How many years do you still have?

Approximately 7,450 people die every day in the United States (2018, United Nations World Population Prospects Report). That's about 2.7 million people per year.

Solomon tells us, "All share a common destiny—the righteous and the wicked, the good and the bad... The same destiny overtakes all...For the living know that they will die" (Ecclesiastes 9:2–5).

George Bernard Shaw affirmed that when he said, "The statistics on death are quite impressive. One out of every one dies."

The fact that we will die is undeniable. So why is it that most of us don't want to acknowledge death, we don't want to discuss it even with the most significant people in our lives, and we hesitate to plan or prepare for it?

Richard Baxter, a Puritan pastor back in the 1600s, wrote a book addressed to pastors in which he charged ministers with the responsibility of preparing their people for death. He wrote, "You have not done well by your people if you have not prepared them to die."

That statement made such an impression upon me that I chose to include the phrase *Prepare to Die* in the title of my book. Not without some reservation, however, I realize that title may not generate sales. No one will say, "I'm dying to read that book."

The seed from which my book title germinated was sown much earlier in my life. It was during the summer following the fourth grade when my buddy Roger and I set out on a Huck Finn–like adventure. We hiked to the Loon Lake Cemetery, an abandoned cemetery worthy of any horror film setting. It had gnarled cedar trees, a creaky wrought iron fence, and grave sites of Civil War soldiers and an entire family massacred in a Sioux Indian uprising. Engraved on one of the tombstones in that graveyard was this eerie epitaph:

Pause, stranger, when you pass me by
As you are now, so once was I
As I am now, so you will be
So prepare for death and follow me

The unsettling words were mesmerizing and haunting. I read them several times. "Prepare for death? Follow me?"...For most of my walk home, I sensed that something was following me. It may have been the first time that I ever gave thought to the fact that I was a mortal being.

Years later I encountered the same epitaph while reading Erwin Lutzer's excellent book *One Minute after You Die*. He presented a witty and wise response to the voice beckoning from the epitaph:

To follow you I'm not content
Until I know which way you went [1]

---

[1] Erwin W. Lutzer, *One Minute After You Die*, (Chicago: Moody Press, 1997) p. 11.

Prepare to die is also a phrase from the popular 1987 comedy *The Princess Bride*. The movie features a character named Inigo Montoya, who is obsessed with avenging his father's death. If he encountered the man who killed his father, he planned to say, "Hello. My name is Inigo Montoya. You killed my father. Prepare to die!" That line is heard so frequently in the movie that it became a favorite for fans to recite.

It is somewhat surprising, however, that nobody explores exactly how one prepares to die. Traditionally, you did it by making peace with God, hence the movie line's occasional substitutes, "Say your prayers!" or "Prepare to meet your Maker!" But the person reciting the line rarely gives their adversary time to prepare.

Jeremy Taylor, an English clergyman in the 1600s writes, "It is a great art to die well." Can you think of someone about whom you would say, "They died well"? What does that even mean? What would that look like?

Aren't you glad that you are reading such an uplifting book? Don't put it down. No one can say,

"This book isn't relevant to me." We are all going to die. Are you prepared and will you die well?

Epicurus, a 4th century BC Greek philosopher and sage, said this: "The art of living well and the art of dying well are one."

You cannot live well if you do not prepare to die well. That is why this book is relevant. There is an additional value in reading this book. I believe this is the topic with which we can engage the unchurched of our society. There is an adage that states, "A broken heart is an open heart." Not always; sometimes people get very bitter and hard hearted in the grieving process. But generally, I would say it's true. A broken heart is open to hearing a word of hope that is graciously delivered with compassion and love. This book contains that hope.

The Faces of Death

We have seen the fact (reality and certainty) of death. Let's consider the faces of death. It is imperative that you understand what follows because I build upon these foundational truths throughout this book.

The Bible speaks of three types of death. There is a common denominator for all three of them. It is the word *separation*. In each of the three ways in which death is spoken of in the Scripture, it always involves separation. [2]

First of all, there is physical death. Physical death is the separation of the soul from the body. The soul, the essential part of who we are, is separated from this earthly tent when our heart stops beating.

It is intriguing that there are nearly 300 euphemisms in the English language for physical death. Many of them arise because we talk so evasively in order to avoid the topic of death. Some of the euphemisms are humorous attempts to blunt the razor's edge of death's reality:

- Assumed room temperature
- Bite the dust
- Bought the farm
- Cashed in one's chips
- Checked out
- Flat lined

---

[2] I am grateful to Dr. David Jeremiah for the outline and insights taken from his teaching message – *"Death: The Fear of Dying"* on "Turning Point."

- Kicked the bucket
- Kicked the oxygen habit
- Left the building
- Met their Maker
- Pushing up daisies
- That was all she wrote

And on and on the list goes. Each one of those expressions is a reference to physical death.

Another form of death that the Bible speaks about is spiritual death. We are all born spiritually dead.

> "As for you, you were dead in your transgressions and sins" (Ephesians 2:1).

Paul is writing to Christians, people who obviously are alive. But he says they were at one point in time dead. Spiritual death is the separation of the soul from God, and when we were born, we were separate from him because of the sinful nature we inherited from Adam. The Bible says, "The wages of sin is death" (Romans 6:23). When sin entered the world through Adam, it was passed on to everyone so that every unregenerate man and woman is dead spiritually—separated from God.

Then there is a third kind of death that is mentioned in the Bible. This is called the *second death*. We read about it in the book of Revelation.

> And I saw the dead, great and small, standing before the throne, and books were opened. Another book was opened, which is the book of life. The dead were judged according to what they had done as recorded in the books...Then death and Hades were thrown into the lake of fire. The lake of fire is the *second death*. Anyone whose name was not found written in the book of life was thrown into the lake of fire (Revelation 20:12–15; all emphasis added).

This last form of death, the second death, is final banishment from God. Spiritual death is the separation of your soul from God. Physical death is the separation of your soul from your body. The second death is the separation of your soul from God forever and ever and ever.

My favorite question: "What do dead people need?"

The answer: They need life. They need to be born again spiritually. That is why Jesus said to Nicodemus, "No one can see the kingdom of God unless they are born again; born from above. You are spiritually dead, Nic. If you are still spiritually dead at the moment of your physical death, you will experience the second death. It is only those who have received me as their Savior that will be made spiritually alive" (My paraphrase of John 3).

Jesus also made the most astounding claim in history, "I am the resurrection and the life. The one who believes in me will live, even though they die (*physically*); and whoever lives by believing in me *will never die*" (John 11:25–26; all emphasis added).

Never die? He is certainly not referring to physical death in that last phrase because believers still die. It is not a reference to spiritual death because we already were dead. Jesus is saying that those who believe in him will not experience the second death.

Thus, if you want to live forever in the presence of God, you must have two birthdays. You have a physical birthday, but you will also need a spiritual birthday. It sounds like a riddle but ponder this: *"If you are only born once, you will have to experience death twice. But if you are born twice, you will only have to think about dying once."* [3]

That's the fact of death and the faces of death. Just a brief word about the fear of death as I bring chapter one to a close.

The Fear of Death

"(Jesus) shared in our humanity so that by his death he might break the power of him who holds the power of death—that is, the devil—and free those who all their lives were *held in slavery by their fear of death*" (Hebrews 2:14-15; all emphasis added).

If you have experienced spiritual rebirth, if you have been made spiritually alive, and you are when you accept Jesus as your Savior, then you should never have to be tormented by the fear of death. The Christian can say, "I am not afraid of death." Perhaps we're fearful of the dying process, but death for a follower of Jesus is not anything to fear. It is only a temporary moment that we walk through to the other side of eternity.

Erwin Lutzer writes:

---

[3] Dr. David Jeremiah, Ibid.

Only on this side of the curtain is death our enemy. Just beyond the curtain the monster turns out to be our friend. The label "Death" is still on the bottle, but the contents are "Life Eternal." Death is our friend because it reminds us that heaven is near. How near? As near as a heartbeat, ...If our eyes could see the spirit world, we might find that we are already at its gates...The tomb is not an entrance to death, but to life. [4]

Now the only way we can know that to be true, the only way that we can have any confidence in such a hope-filled declaration is by being able to put our finger on a Scripture text. It's only by the Word of God that we understand anything about the afterlife. There are many fears and misconceptions regarding what lies beyond death's door. So I'll close this chapter with one of the great verses offering us reassurance.

For we know that when this earthly tent we live in is taken down (that is, when we die and leave this earthly body), we will have a house in heaven,

---

[4] Erwin W. Lutzer, Ibid, p. 77–78.

an eternal body made for us by God
himself and not by human hands
(2 Corinthians 5:1).

That verse begins with a phrase filled with significance: "For we know." You never read Paul saying, "Got my fingers crossed on this. I'm not quite sure about this, but boy, wouldn't it be cool if this were the case." No, he uses unambiguous definitive language, "We know." Philosophical speculation provides no comfort other than a delusional comfort. Paul writes of that which we as followers of Jesus can embrace and hold on to with great confidence.

Insight and Inspiration:

I know that my Redeemer liveth,
And on the earth again shall stand;
I know eternal life He giveth,
That grace and power are in His hand.

I know His promise never faileth;
The word He speaks, it cannot die;
Though cruel death my flesh assaileth,
Yet I shall see Him by and by.

I know my mansion He prepareth,

That where He is there I may be;
O wondrous thought, for me He careth,
And He at last will come for me.[5]

> Who hasn't wondered, "What happens after death?" It would be both unreasonable and foolish to live your entire life never considering and being unprepared for an event that we all know is inevitable. The mortality rate on earth is 100 percent.
>
> —Rick Warren

> We cannot love to live if we cannot bear to die.
>
> —William Penn

> Be absolute for death; either death or life shall thereby be the sweeter."
>
> —William Shakespeare

---

[5] Jessie Brown, *I Know my Redeemer Liveth*, first published in 1893. The title is based upon Job 19:25.

Chapter 2

Peaceful Sleep

I t has been my honor on many occasions to officiate at a graveside service at Fort Snelling National Cemetery. It is always a sobering sight, a sacred moment; over 200,000 white stone markers stand at attention in precisely placed rows. The headstones remember individuals who served this country in the military, perhaps even lives lost in combat. Or the headstones may be for spouses who made their own sacrifices by being separated from loved ones as they served. Fort Snelling National Cemetery is a graphic reminder that there is a price to be paid for freedom. Each date of death engraved on the stone markers also bears testimony to the fragility and fleetingness of life.

In military honors, the gun salute is followed by the playing of "Taps." Since 1862, the time of the Civil

War, "Taps" has been played at military funerals to honor the sacrifice of fallen service members. Twenty-four melancholy notes that evoke tearful emotions. The lyrics of "Taps" begin:

Day is done, gone the sun
From the lake, from the hill, from the sky
All is well, safely rest. God is nigh.
Go to sleep, peaceful sleep,
May the soldier or sailor, God keep.
On the land or the deep, Safe in sleep.

"Go to sleep, peaceful sleep,...Safe in sleep?" Is sleep simply another euphemism intended to shield us from the harsh reality of death? Is it just one more expression to add to the euphemism list in chapter 1?

Laid to Rest

Graveside services are referred to as "laying someone to rest." That is a profoundly beautiful and comforting expression when it is understood. Its origin is found in the language from the era of the biblical writers. In the Greek language, the language that the New Testament was originally written in, the word *koimeteria*— sleeping place, carried over into our language as cemetery. You can hear the word *coma* in the Greek verb *koiman*—to put to sleep. At a graveside service the body is laid to rest in its final resting place.

Time and again the phrase that is used in the New Testament for the death of an individual is the expression *fallen asleep*. It is very likely that the early Church learned to use this phrase from the example of Jesus himself. To the funeral mourners at the synagogue leader's home he said, "The girl is not dead but asleep" (Matthew 9:24). After hearing the news of Lazarus's death, he told the disciples, "Our friend Lazarus has fallen asleep; but I am going there to wake him up" (John 11:11).

Paul uses the same figure of speech in 1 Corinthians 15, that magnificent chapter about the significance of Jesus's resurrection. He uses it again in 1 Thessalonians 4 in a foundational passage for our understanding of grief and what happens when death occurs. We will walk through those verses in the next chapter.

Laid to rest and *fallen asleep* reflect the view of the authors of Scripture that death is like sleep. Perhaps the term *sleep* is used because of the appearance of the body. The stillness of the body at death resembles sleep. But the primary association is that sleep is temporary. Just as your body arose from the bed this morning when the alarm clock sounded, so also, the body that has been laid to rest will one day rise from its resting place.

Philip Yancey describes a faith-inspired epitaph that marks the grave of a grandmother who lies in a church cemetery in rural Louisiana. In accordance with the woman's instructions, only one word is engraved upon the stone. The word is *Waiting.* [6]

Waiting for what? Waiting for the return of Jesus and the resurrection of the body that will occur at that glorious moment.

The psalmist writes, "When I awake, I will see you face to face and be satisfied" (Psalm 17:15; NLT). That verse can be viewed from the perspective of the body that has been laid to rest in the grave awaiting its resurrection. When the body awakens from its resting place at the Second Coming of Jesus, it will see him face-to-face and be satisfied.

---

[6] Philip Yancey, *The Jesus I Never Knew*, (Grand Rapids: Zondervan, 1995), 364.

The Immortal Soul

Physical death is the separation of the soul from the body. So what happens to the soul at the moment of death? And what exactly is the soul?

John Ortberg, in his must-read book *Soul Keeping: Caring for the Most Important Part of You*, cites Jeffrey Boyd, who is a Yale psychiatrist, an ordained minister, and coauthor of *Diagnostic and Statistical Manual of Mental Disorders*. About half of church attenders adopt what Boyd calls the Looney Tunes Theory of the soul. He elaborates upon what he means by that by recalling a cartoon scene in which Daffy Duck is blown up by dynamite after which a translucent image of Daffy Duck floats up from the dead body. The image has wings and carries a harp. [7]

One accurate aspect of the cartoon is that we are a body-soul union. We learn that from the very opening pages of the Bible. In Genesis, God formed Adam's body from the dust of the earth and God then breathed into his nostrils and he became a living soul. (The KJ and ASV translate the Hebrew

---

[7] John Ortberg, *Soul Keeping: Caring for the Most Important Part of You*, (Grand Rapids: Zondervan, 2014), 28-29. Ortberg cites *"If Daffy Duck were"*: Jeffrey Boyd, *Soul Psychology* (Colorado Springs: Soul esearch Institute,1994), 59.

word *nephesh* in Genesis 2:7 as soul. Other versions may note that in their footnotes.)

As part of the aftermath of the man and woman's choice to disobey in the Garden, God pronounced, "For dust you are and to dust you will return" (Genesis 3:19). That is not a verse that gets crocheted on pillowcases at nursing homes. No one stencils that verse on the family room wall. But we will experience physical death and the body will return to dust. We are not, however, just "Dust in the Wind" as the old Kansas rock group song title stated. The soul, the essential part of who we are, lives on.

Our soul is made by God and for God and in need of God. That is why the neglected soul is spoken of in the Bible as being thirsty and hungry and weary and lost and unsatisfied. It is why we still feel empty and sense that something is missing even when our lives are filled with activities and noise to mask that emptiness. If only our eyes saw souls instead of bodies, how different our prioritizing of life would be.

George MacDonald, the Scottish author, poet, and Christian minister, said, "Never tell a child, you have a soul. Teach him, you are a soul; you have a body."

Reflect for a moment upon this verse from Henry Wadsworth Longfellow's poem "A Psalm of Life." He composed the poem shortly after the death of his first wife. Imagine the comfort that this truth brought him.

Life is real! Life is earnest!
And the grave is not its goal;
"Dust thou art, to dust returnest,"
Was not spoken of the soul.[8]

The soul is immortal. At the moment of death, our soul does not sleep. The soul of a follower of Jesus is ushered immediately into the joy of his presence.

In stark contrast to this belief is the view of the outspoken atheist Christopher Hitchens, who died in 2011 from pneumonia related to the cancer he had been battling. During his lengthy medical treatment doctors would advise Mr. Hitchens that his body wasn't responding to treatment and that his body was failing. In his book *Mortality*, he recounts

---

[8] Henry Wadsworth Longfellow, *A Psalm of Life*. First published in 1838.

his reaction to his doctors' statements. Hitchens's response was, "I don't have a body. I am a body." Just a body and nothing more.

When Sir Michael Faraday, a scientist and a Christian, was dying, some journalists questioned him as to his speculations about life after death. "Speculations?" he replied. "I know nothing about speculations. I'm resting on certainties. I know that my Redeemer liveth, and because He lives, I shall live also."

On what is such an inspiring statement of conviction based? Can we put our finger on a text?

"Yes, we are fully confident, and we would rather be away from these earthly bodies, for then we will be at home with the Lord. To be absent from the body is to be present with the Lord" (2 Corinthians 5:8).

Slow down and read that verse again. What is it that is away from the earthly body? Paul is talking about that moment of physical death when the soul is separated from the body. At death, the body is laid to rest, but the soul will be ushered into the presence of God in heaven.

In Luke's account of the crucifixion, one of the thieves crucified alongside Jesus said, "Jesus, remember me when you come into your kingdom." Jesus answered him, "Truly I tell you, today you will be with me in paradise" (see Luke 23:42–43).

"Today [i.e., immediately upon your physical death, while your body is still hanging on the cross] you [i.e., your soul] will be with me in paradise."

An epitaph on a tombstone somewhere in the Northwest humorously captures and summarizes these truths:

> Here lies the body of old man Peas,
> buried beneath the flowers and trees.
> But Peas ain't here, just the pod. Peas
> shelled out and went to God.

This hope is expressed rather eloquently in a story about Winston Churchill. He had planned his own funeral, which took place in Saint Paul's Cathedral in London. The funeral included many of the great hymns of the church. At his request, at the conclusion of the service, a bugler positioned high in the dome of Saint Paul's played "Taps." Then as the mournful sound of "Taps" subsided, another bugler placed on the other side of the great dome sounded "Reveille"—"It's time to get up. It's time to get up. It's time to get up in the morning."

Churchill knew that life did not end with a long slow ride in a hearse. Death is not the end but the beginning of something wonderful and unimaginable. He knew a new and beautiful world would dawn when he closed his eyes in death. His soul would leave his earthly tent and enter into its heavenly home.

Contrast the conviction and comfort that Churchill experienced with the beliefs expressed in a very popular funeral poem. The poem is narrated from the perspective of the deceased person who encourages mourners to not cry at their grave.

Do not stand on my grave and weep
I am not there I do not sleep.
I am a thousand winds that blow
I am the diamond glints in the snow
I am the sunlight on ripened grain
I am a gentle autumn's rain
When you awaken in the morning hush
I am the swift uplifting rush
I am the birds in circled flight
I am the soft stars that shine at night

So do not stand on my grave and cry
I am not there...I did not die [9]

Blah, blah, blah. The poem's minimization of grief and denial of the reality of death is built upon the New Age belief that our spirit merges with an impersonal creation at death. And that is supposed to be comforting? Really? In my cynical moments, I insert these lines into the middle of the poem:

I am the mucus in your nose,
I am the fungus between your toes.

I don't want to mock the person who tries to find comfort in the poem. Truthfully, I feel a genuine sense of sadness over the empty deception they embrace. My added lines, however, are logically consistent with the pantheistic tenets of New Age religion upon which the poem is based.

The term *New Age* is thrown around quite a bit. What does it entail? New Age thinking is:
- Pantheistic—a belief that identifies God with creation or regards nature as a manifestation of an impersonal God.

---

[9] The poem is of uncertain authorship. It is variously attributed to Anonymous, Melinda Sue Pacho, and Mary Elizabeth Frye.

- Mystical—a view that maintains that truth is something one finds within oneself. Therefore, truth is relative and there are no universal absolutes.
- Syncretistic—a blending and merging of religious ideas. New Age has much in common with Hinduism and ancient Gnosticism.

The poem is clearly contrary to what the Bible teaches about death and the afterlife. Let's return once more to the Biblical analogy of death being like sleep to find the comfort in that truth. Imagine a child tucked into bed by their mother on Christmas Eve. The child is filled with anticipation and excitement knowing that they will awaken to gifts around the tree. They sleep peacefully, however, because of their assurance of their parents' love and goodness.

I will extend that analogy at a graveside service and remind the family that the beloved mother who tucked them into bed so many times is now being laid to rest by her children. Our comfort in that moment is based on our assurance that she will awaken to and rise to indescribable goodness. Our confidence of that hope is founded upon our Heavenly Father's love and goodness for us.

But Wait! There's More

I will conclude this chapter with another word picture that I occasionally use at a graveside service. In those mind-consuming moments of grief, people retain this simple illustration.

Remember the name Ron Popeil? Ron Popeil was the marketing personality for Ronco Corporation; he pitched the Veg-O-Matic, the Dice-O-Matic, the Popeil pocket fisherman, and the amazing spray hair in a can. But Ron Popeil's greatest creation wasn't any of those products. It was the tagline that invariably popped up in his late-night television infomercials. His spiel and appeal were always followed by his signature catchphrase: "But wait! There's more!" No matter how tantalizing his offer was, there was the promise: "But wait! There's more!"

What a fitting thought for that moment when the body is laid to rest. "But wait! There's more!" Our good God has told us and reassured us that there is more beyond this life for his children. Continue to read, and you will receive clarification on what exactly "more" is.

Insight and Inspiration:

Explain why the soul feels its worth in the Christmas carol "O Holy Night".
O holy night the stars are brightly shining
It is the night of our dear Savior's birth
Long lay the world in sin and error pining
Till He appeared and the soul felt its worth

For many generations, when parents would tuck their children into bed, they would have them recite a little prayer. My mother taught me this:

Now I lay me down to sleep,
I pray the Lord my Soul to keep;
If I should die before I 'wake,
I pray the Lord my Soul to take.

There is a second verse to that prayer:

Our days begin with trouble here,
our life is but a span.
And cruel death is always near,
so frail a thing is man.

Do you hear that prayer any differently after reading this chapter?

Multitudes who sleep in the dust of the earth will awake: some to everlasting life, others to shame and everlasting contempt (Daniel 12:2).

Chapter 3

No Hope, False Hope, or Living Hope

One of the most touching and tearful scenes in the movie *Forrest Gump* occurs at Jenny's grave. Forrest says, "Mama always said that dyin' was a part of life. I sure wish it wasn't."

That scene was so sad. We grieved because Jenny was such a tormented soul from the abuse and injustice in her past. We grieved with Forrest as we sensed the heart-shattering agony of his loss. Grief related to the death of a loved one is such a consuming and excruciating emotion. It is a universal emotion in this fallen world, and yet a Christian's experience of grief should be different.

"Brothers and sisters, we do not want you to be uninformed about those who sleep in death, so that you do not grieve like the rest of mankind, who have no hope" (1 Thessalonians 4:13).

That is one of the saddest expressions in the Scripture—grieving with no hope. To grieve without hope of there being something more beyond the grave is an unbearable despair.

There are three groups of people in this world. What differentiates them from one another is the word *hope*. There are some who have no hope.

No Hope

An atheist believes nothing exists beyond the moment of death. You live, you die; the candle goes out. Nothing remains. You were just a biological organism that ceased functioning. How depressing!

Bertrand Russell, the British philosopher and author of a book entitled *Why I am Not a Christian*, gives the classic statement of atheism. He wrote, "I believe that when I die, I shall rot."

Ol' Bert probably wasn't a fun guy to party with. His statement, however, is the honest and logically consistent conclusion to an atheistic view of life. There is no hope of life beyond the moment of death. Anticipating his own death, Russell said, "There is darkness without and when I die there will be darkness within. There is no splendor, no vastness anywhere, only triviality for a moment and then nothing."

Ernest Hemingway held the same empty belief. He said, "Life is just a dirty trick, a short journey from nothingness to nothingness."

There is no comfort or hope in that view of death. You live, and then you die. You simply cease to exist at the moment of death.

My favorite Russell quote is, "Most people would rather die than think; many do." But behind his statement is the intellectual arrogance that is so prevalent in atheism. You can detect the need to smugly mock a caricature of Christian faith. In claiming to be wise, they became fools (see Romans 1:22).

Behind Russell's statement is also an inaccurate definition of faith captured in Voltaire critical remark, "Faith consists in believing what reason cannot." Mark Twain expressed it this way, "Faith is believing what you know ain't so." Those definitions produce phrases such as blind faith and leap of faith.

False Hope

"Faith," writes Thomas Edison, "as well intentioned as it may be, must be built on facts, not fiction—faith in fiction is a damnable *false hope.*"

The essential aspect of faith is not the fervency with which someone embraces their beliefs; it is also not the amount of faith that they claim to possess. The crucial issue in faith is the truthfulness and trustworthiness of the object that faith is placed in. As Friedrich Nietzsche noted, "A casual stroll through the lunatic asylum shows that faith does not prove anything."

Faith in false hope is prevalent throughout our society and manifested in various belief systems:

- Reincarnation—a repeating cycle of birth and death and rebirth, known as samsara, to address one's karma. Adherents to eastern religions believe one escapes samsara through obtaining an enlightened state of

consciousness called nirvana. The word *nirvana* literally means "the blowing out."
- Pantheism—at death our spirit merges with an impersonal universe and we become one with the universe.
- Works-oriented religions that believe eternal bliss is granted if you are good enough to gain God's approval. But by what standard do you measure goodness? Can you ever be certain that you are good enough?

False hope is far worse than no hope. People who find themselves confronted by hopeless despair may be inclined to search until they find truth they can base their faith on and thereby have genuine hope. Those who have false hope are like the foolish man who built his house on the sand. That is Jesus's parable in Matthew 7. When the storms of life come, when death occurs, a foolish man discovers too late that his hope was built on a faulty foundation.

Psychologist Carl Jung said, "No one can live in peace in a house that he knows shortly will tumble about his ears." A very insightful statement for a man with such an angst-ridden soul; Jung sought for answers in Spiritism and in the demonic realm.

Here is a homework assignment: ask someone this question, "What do you believe happens when you die?" Their answer will reveal what they have placed their faith in. Everyone has placed their faith in something.

Living Hope

Peter writes of a third hope, "Praise be to the God and Father of our Lord Jesus Christ! In his great mercy he has given us new birth into a living hope through the resurrection of Jesus Christ from the dead, and into an inheritance that can never perish, spoil or fade. This inheritance is kept in heaven for you" (1 Peter 1:3–4).

As followers of Jesus, we recognize that the resurrection of Jesus is the pivotal event in human history. In that empty tomb on Easter morning is a triumphal statement by God that the best is yet to come. We believe in the immortality of the soul and in the resurrection of the body because Jesus was raised from the dead. There will be release from these aging bodies and the glory of heaven awaits us. We look forward to a city whose builder and maker is God (Hebrews 11:10).

Billy Graham confidently communicated this hope when he said, "Someday you will read or hear that Billy Graham is dead. Don't you believe a word of it. I shall be more alive than I am now. I will just have changed my address. I will have gone into the presence of God."

Writing about the connection between Jesus's resurrection and our hope, Paul penned this truth, "And if Christ has not been raised, your faith is futile; you are still in your sins. Then those also who have fallen asleep in Christ are lost. If only for this life we have hope in Christ, we are of all people most to be pitied" (1 Corinthians 15:17–19).

Paul is saying, "If the resurrection of Jesus did not occur, Bertrand Russell is right. We would have no hope."

Elaborating upon why a Christian can grieve with hope, Paul pens the classic passage found in 1 Thessalonians 4:13–18. In six verses, he presents the foundation of our hope. I will walk through the passage briefly.

> Brothers and sisters, we do not want
> you to be uninformed about those

who sleep in death, so that you do not
grieve like the rest of mankind, who
have no hope (1 Thessalonians 4:13).

Note first of all the distinction which exists between
those to whom Paul speaks to and about. There are
the "brothers and sisters," and then there is "the
rest of mankind, who have no hope." A clear distinction is drawn. "Brothers and sisters" is a reference to followers of Jesus. We will say, "Hey Bro!" to
anyone today, but biblically that term applies only
to those who have placed their faith in Jesus.

That distinction is not a superficial one. It is a vital
delineation. It is the dividing line between faith and
unbelief, hope and hopelessness, being spiritually
alive or spiritually dead. There is no middle terri-
tory. We are either brothers and sisters in Christ,
or we are part of the rest of mankind without hope
and without God. If we are not clear on that differentiation, we will be confused and lack any sense
of assurance, any certitude regarding what Paul is
about to say regarding death and grief.

One thing that is troubling to me is when I hear
someone say, "I've always been a Christian." No,
you haven't! Perhaps what you mean is that you

have grown up with a strong tradition of attending church. From the time you were a little child, you remember involvement in church. All that means, however, is that you are a churchgoer. To be a Christian, there was a moment in time when you received Jesus as your Savior, and at that moment God made you spiritually alive and you became his child.

We hear people say, "We are all God's children." No, we are not! All of us are his creation, but we *become* his children. John writes, "Yet to all who did receive him, to those who believed in his name, he gave the right to become children of God" (John 1:12).

There are three operative verbs in that verse— receive, believe, and become. We *become* God's child at that moment in time when we *believe* we need a Savior and we *receive* Jesus and his gift of forgiveness. Again, if we lack clarity and conviction in this matter, death will be a fearful enemy.

What is our basis for hope as we stand by a grave? Paul explains by pointing back in time and then pointing forward. He points back to the resur- rection of Jesus. He anchors our future hope of heaven in that historical event in the past. Jesus's resurrection is proof that we too will live. Jesus rose so we have a living hope and, therefore, we don't grieve like the rest of mankind, who have no hope.

> For we believe that Jesus died and rose again, and so we believe that God will bring with Jesus those who have fallen asleep in him (4:14).

When Jesus comes again, (there are over 300 references to his return in the New Testament), he will bring with him the souls of all believers throughout time. We are building upon the foundation laid in the first two chapters. Remember, physical death is the separation of the soul from the body. The body is laid to rest, but the soul was ushered into the presence of God.

> According to the Lord's word, we tell you that we who are still alive, who are left until the coming of the Lord, will certainly not precede those who have fallen asleep. For the Lord himself will come down from heaven, with a loud command, with the voice of the archangel and with the trumpet call of God,

and the dead in Christ will rise first (4:15–16).

The body will rise from its resting place; it will be recreated and reunited with the soul. I can't comprehend that, but I know that the One who spoke the universe into existence can certainly bring it to pass.

> After that, we who are still alive and are left will be caught up together with them in the clouds to meet the Lord in the air (4:17).

The event in verse 17 is known as the rapture. Jesus is coming back for his people. That is why we have hope!

Paul writes, "We are eagerly waiting for him to return as our Savior. He will take our weak mortal bodies and change them into glorious bodies like his own, using the same power with which he will bring everything under his control" (Philippians 3:20–21; NLT).

So here's the sequence at the coming of Jesus for his Church. At the moment of his coming, all those who have died throughout history who have placed their faith in God will be resurrected from the grave and their souls will be joined to the newly redone bodies. That is the ultimate extreme makeover. Immediately after that event and probably almost simultaneous to it, there will be a total transformation of believers who are alive at the moment of Jesus's return. Paul writes:

> Listen, I tell you a mystery: We will not all sleep, but we will all be changed—in a flash, in the twinkling of an eye, at the last trumpet. For the trumpet will sound, the dead will be raised imperishable, and we will be changed. For the perishable must clothe itself with the imperishable, and the mortal with immortality (I Corinthians 15:51–53).

To quote J.M. Barrie's character Peter Pan, "To die will be an awfully big adventure."

> And so we will be with the Lord forever. Therefore encourage one another with these words (4:17b,18).

What is the encouragement? In part, it is the joy of knowing that on that day there is going to be a reunion with family members who have passed from this life. Your heart has been aching so long because you miss them so much. But you will see them again if they were followers of Jesus and if you also know Jesus as your Savior.

Rest and rejoice in the balm of that reassurance as found in the hymn "It is Well with my Soul." The traumatic and painful background story that inspired this hymn's composition is frequently retold. Horatio Spafford penned the lyrics as he coped with the loss of his four daughters. He clung to the hope of his Christian faith expressed in and through these lyrics:

> But, Lord, 'tis for thee, for thy coming we wait,
>
> The sky, not the grave, is our goal,
>
> Oh trump of the angel! Oh voice of the Lord!
>
> Blessed hope, blessed rest of my soul!

And Lord, haste the day when my faith
shall be sight,

The clouds be rolled back as a scroll;

The trumpet shall sound, and the Lord
shall descend,

Even so, it is well with my soul. [10]

Insight and Inspiration:

"Death is not a period that ends the great sentence of life, but a comma that punctuates it to more lofty significance. Death is not a blind alley that leads the human race into a state of nothingness, but an open door which leads man into life eternal."—Martin Luther King Jr., "Eulogy for the Martyred Children"

"Death is no more than passing from one room into another. But there's a difference for me, you know. Because in that other room I shall be able to see."—Helen Keller

Late in his life, President John Quincy Adams was asked how he was doing. Here is how he answered,

---

[10] *It is Well with My Soul,* Horatio Spafford, first published in 1876.

"John Quincy Adams is well, sir, very well. The house in which he has been living is feeble, the shingles are coming off the roof, the foundation is a bit shaky and he has received word from its Maker that he must vacate soon. But Mr. Adams is fine, sir, just fine."

"I have formed during the last few years such close relationships with this best and truest friend of mankind that death's image is not only no longer terrifying to me, but is indeed very soothing and consoling, and I thank my God for graciously granting me the opportunity...of learning that death is the key which unlocks the door to our true happiness."—Wolfgang Amadeus Mozart

He will wipe every tear from their eye. There will be no more death or mourning or crying or pain, for the old order of things has passed away (Revelation 21:4).

Chapter 4

Numbering Our Days

B enjamin Franklin's resting place is located in Christ Church Cemetery in Philadelphia. As a basis for review of the first three chapters, let's evaluate an epitaph he composed for himself when he was 22 years old. An epitaph, literally "on the grave" in ancient Greek, is text honoring the dead. Franklin's actual gravestone simply reads, "Benjamin and Deborah Franklin" while the epitaph he penned as a young man is displayed on a plaque close by. It reads and appears like this:

The Body of
B. Franklin, Printer,
Like the Cover of an old Book,
Its Contents torn out,
And Stript of its Lettering and Gilding,
Lies here, Food for Worms.

But the Work shall not be lost;
For it will, as he believe'd,
appear once more
In a new and more elegant Edition,
Corrected and improved
By the Author.

At death the body, *the Cover of the old Book,* is laid to rest in the grave. The contents of the book, *its Lettering and Gilding,* the soul of the believer, passes immediately to be with the Lord. Physical death is the separation of the soul from the body. But the body will *appear once more*, it will be raised at the Second Coming of Jesus. It will be transformed and reunited with the soul that returns with Jesus. The body will then appear in *a new and more elegant Edition, Corrected and improved By the Author,* the Author of Life, God our Creator.

That was a bit of summary of the first three chapters. We need the anchor of those foundational truths in order to die in peace. That biblical perspective on death then allows us to live more purposefully and intentionally.

In this chapter we will reflect upon Psalm 90. Moses is the author of this psalm. We don't know the exact historical setting that prompted his writing, but an intriguing suggestion is Numbers chapter 20. Three very significant events occur in that chapter— Moses' sister Miriam dies, his brother Aaron dies, and God tells Moses that he won't be allowed to enter the Promised Land.

In the midst of the heartache and pain of that season of his life, Moses may have composed this psalm. If the psalm is prompted by that chapter in his life, I find the words he penned even weightier. While we can receive inspiration from people when they are on the mountain top, we generally glean the deepest insights from those who share their wisdom from having gone through the dark valleys.

> Psalm 90
> A prayer of Moses the man of God.
> [1] Lord, you have been our dwelling place
> throughout all generations.
> [2] Before the mountains were born
> or you brought forth the whole world,
> from everlasting to everlasting
> you are God.
> [3] You turn people back to dust,
> saying, "Return to dust, you mortals."

View those words through the lens of having just buried a brother and a sister. There is a submission to the reality of our powerlessness in those words. In this life there is so much that is out of our control. This is a Serenity Prayer moment—"God, grant me the serenity to accept the things I cannot change." That statement and verse 3 are an acknowledgment that we are not the sovereign masters of our lives.

> [4] A thousand years in your sight
> are like a day that has just gone by,
> or like a watch in the night.
> [5] Yet you sweep people away in the sleep of death—
> they are like the new grass of the morning:
> [6] In the morning it springs up new,
> but by evening it is dry and withered.

Feeling encouraged and uplifted yet? We are like grass; as time passes, we dry and wither. As someone said, "Time is a great healer, but a very poor beautician."

> [10] Our days may come to seventy years,
> or eighty, if our strength endures;

yet the best of them are but trouble
and sorrow,
for they quickly pass, and we fly away.

Now verse 12 is a prayer request, the first of two
very significant requests in the psalm. The request
is a foundational building block in living life
purposefully.

> [12] Teach us to number our days,
> that we may gain a heart of wisdom.

Question: What is the wisdom we gain if we learn
to number our days?

Robert Fulghum wrote a book entitled *Everything
I Need to Know I Learned in Kindergarten*. I have no
idea what the book is about because the title strikes
me as being so silly that I've never considered
reading the book. Perhaps it is very good; however,
most of the deeper lessons on how to live life well
are learned in the classroom of suffering, or in the
classroom of waiting, or in the classroom of broken
relationships, or in the classroom of death. They
can be hard and cruel instructors. They are also
lifelong courses far beyond kindergarten. You don't
ever graduate during this life, and far too many get

stuck in the pain and miss the wisdom and growth these instructors bring.

Just what is a heart of wisdom? In the Old Testament, wisdom is not theoretical, but it is practical. A wise person is not the academic with a brain stuffed with facts; it is someone who is skillful at living life well. Back to the question: What is the wisdom we gain if we learn to number our days? What are the lessons learned? Let me offer two broad overarching answers. Firstly, a wise heart understands:

The Fleetingness and the Impermanence of Life

A reoccurring theme lamented by poets and songwriters alike is the inability to hold back the sands of time. When our hourglass runs out of sand, we can't flip it over and start again. How quickly life passes by. When Lennon and McCartney recorded "When I'm 64," I was only 13. Now I can sing, "When I *was* 64."

As we learn to number our days, we drop the illusion of permanence and embrace our mortality. Solomon writes, "...for death is the destiny of everyone; the living should take this to heart" (Ecclesiastes 7:2).

That is why in the conclusion of Ecclesiastes, he addresses young people. He writes, "Remember your Creator while you are still young" (Ecclesiastes 12:1). In other words, get these matters of life and death and eternity sorted out while time appears to be on your side because despite the insistence of the Bible in these matters, despite the undeniable reality of our mortality, most attempt to avoid any thought of death at all, particularly the prospect of their own.

That is why Moses prays, "Teach us to number our days" even though he has been wandering in the wilderness for forty years where an entire generation of people died. It's estimated that 15,000 people died annually in that 40-year trek around the desert. Funeral after funeral after funeral, day after day after day, and yet, they still needed to internalize the impermanence of life.

Secondly, a wise heart understands:

The Significance and Urgency of Caring for the Soul

Nike Company promoted their products with the commercial caption: "Life is short! Just do it!" The question becomes, "What is the *it* we are supposed to just do?" If *it* is merely bouncing around in new tennis shoes, that doesn't seem very significant or inspiring.

I came across this statement by John Maxwell: "You cannot overestimate the unimportance of almost everything." You must think about that statement. Read it again and pause.

Wayne Dyer wrote, "There are two rules for living in harmony. #(1) Don't sweat the small stuff, and #(2) It's all small stuff." Dyer directed that comment to Richard Carlson in a letter. It became the inspiration for Richard Carlson's book title: *Don't Sweat the Small Stuff...and It's All Small Stuff.* The book was a *New York Times* #1 bestseller.[11]

But it is not all small stuff! Yes, much of what gets our undies in a bundle is insignificant. We may get bent out of shape over the most trivial and inconsequential matters. But some things have eternal significance, like the condition and the state of your soul! The wise heart understands that. That was a reoccurring theme in Jesus's teaching.

---

[11] Richard Carlson, *Don't Sweat the Small Stuff*, (New York: Hyperion, 1997), p. 3.

And Jesus told them a parable, saying, "The land of a rich man was very productive. And he began reasoning to himself, saying, 'What shall I do, since I have no place to store my crops?' Then he said, 'This is what I will do: I will tear down my barns and build larger ones, and there I will store all my grain and my goods. And I will say to my soul, "Soul, you have many goods laid up for many years to come; take your ease, eat, drink and be merry."' But God said to him, 'You fool! This very night your soul is required of you; and now who will own what you have prepared?' So is the man who stores up treasure for himself and is not rich toward God." (Luke 12:16–21; NASB)

All the lessons from Psalm 90 are in that parable—the reminder of the impermanence of life, the need for wisdom to number our days, the warning against misplaced priorities, and the ultimate primacy and urgency of tending to the eternal state of your soul.

"Teach us to number our days," is a reality check prayer. It can be a wake-up call that will cause us to view life differently and, therefore, prompt us to change course in life. Sometimes in that wake-up call we write a bucket list—a list of things that we want to experience or achieve before we kick the bucket.

That expression came into wide use following the release of the 2007 film *Bucket List*, starring Jack Nicholson and Morgan Freeman. The story line is about two terminally ill men who make a wish list of things they want to do before they kick the bucket, and so they take a road trip.

The phrase *bucket list* can be paired with the Latin expression *carpe diem.* That is another phrase popularized by a movie, *Dead Poets Society*. In that film Professor Keating (Robin Williams) inspired his students with the phrase *carpe diem*—seize the day, make the most of every moment with creativity and passion.

Carpe diem is a reminder to live fully present and to experience the pleasures of life. Eat dessert first. Life is too short, too uncertain to play it safe. That can be a needed reminder. Where did we ever get the idea that Christians are supposed to be stoic, dour-faced bores who don't enjoy life? However, a life spent only seizing moments and crossing things off a bucket list can be a life of folly if your bucket list does not consider the coming of Jesus, to whom we must give an account.

Almost universally when people look back on their lives, they wish their priorities had been different. Evaluate life while you still have a chance to make important changes. Complete these sentences:

"If I could do it all again, I would _____."

"If I could rewrite the script, I would _____."

"If I had my life to live over, this is what I'd do differently _____."

Press pause to evaluate. Did any of your answers reflect the need to tend to the eternal state of your soul? If not, you have answered like a fool. This life is not a dress rehearsal; we don't get a second shot at it. This prayer really can be a reset button—"Lord, teach me to number my days, that I may gain a heart of wisdom."

Insight and Inspiration:

> Our lives are ever on the way
> And Death is ever nigh.
> The moment when our lives begin
> We all begin to die.
> > —A grave marker near
> > Barrington, Vermont, 1792

> "Is this the little girl I carried? Is this
> the little boy at play? I don't remember
> growing older...when did they?"
> > —Tevye, *Fiddler on the Roof*

Evaluate and explain these statements in light of each other:

> "The unexamined life is not worth living."
> > —Socrates

> "An unplanned life is not worth examining."
> > —Aristotle

> "Anything less than a conscious com-
> mitment to the important is an

unconscious commitment to the
unimportant."

—Stephen Covey

Be very careful, then, how you live—
not as unwise but as wise, making the
most of every opportunity, because the
days are evil (Ephesians 5:15-16).

Chapter 5

Leaving a Lasting Legacy

Management guru Stephen Covey wrote a book several years ago entitled *First Things First.* It's like a handbook for living a more productive life. Covey proposed that the purpose of life could be summed up in four essential points, all of them beginning with the letter L. The purpose of life is to live, to love, to learn, and to leave a legacy. [12]

It is the topic of leaving a legacy that we turn to in this chapter. We will look again at Psalm 90. I had mentioned that there are two significant prayer requests in the psalm that are pertinent to living and dying well. It is the second request we will focus on now.

---

[12] Stephen Covey, A. Roger Merrill, and Rebecca R. Merrill, *First Things First: To Live, to Love, to Learn, to Leave a Legacy.* (New York: Simon and Schuster), 1994.

As we continue, I want you to consider the word picture of a clock and a compass. It is a word picture found in Covey's book. In our efforts to put first things first, we can receive insight from reflecting on the purpose of these two instruments.

The Clock

The clock represents our appointments, our schedules, our to-do lists, and what we do with time. The clock is also an hourglass that reminds us of the brevity of life. The clock is very apparent in Psalm 90. Moses wrote:

> Our days may come to seventy years,
> or eighty, if our strength endures;
> ...(Psalm 90:10).

That awareness of the brevity and impermanence of life led to the first prayer request:

> Teach us to number our days, that we may gain a heart of wisdom (Psalm 90:12).

That request then leads logically to the second petition:

> May the favor of the Lord our God rest on us; establish[13] the work of our hands for us—yes, establish[14] the work of our hands (Psalm 90:17).

The repetition of the request in verse 12 adds weight to it. Moses is pleading with God that his life would count for something. He wanted to leave an enduring legacy.

I am not using the term *legacy* in the legal sense of a bequest in a will. That is an inheritance, the material possessions we leave to our children. Craig Lounsbrough highlighted the difference between an inheritance and a legacy when he wrote, "An inheritance is what you leave *with* people. A legacy is what you leave *in* them."

That distinction has been recognized for millennia. Pericles, an ancient Greek statesman born around 495 BC, wrote, "What you leave behind is not what is engraved in stone monuments, but what is woven into the lives of others."

---

[13] Or *give permanence to* (NASB).

[14] Ibid.

The reality is every life leaves a legacy. Some leave positive and transformative marks on the lives of others. Some people leave scars. In the Motown classic "Papa was a Rollin' Stone," The Temptations recount the life of Papa who made his home wherever he laid his hat at the end of the day. When Papa died his children remorsefully reminisce, "All he left us was alone." Papa didn't leave an inheritance behind, but he left a legacy of children struggling with abandonment issues.

The Compass

The compass in our word picture represents our vision, our mission, and our life direction. That is, of course, crucial to the legacy we leave. The question everyone needs to ask themselves is, "What type of legacy do I want to leave, and is my life pointed in the right direction to leave that kind of legacy?"

The second half of that question is emphasized in a statement by James Cabell. He comments, "While it is well enough to leave footprints on the sands of time, it is even more important to make sure they point in a commendable direction."

As we age, sobering thoughts about life's brevity and death's certainty (v10, 12) cause us to wonder how we will be remembered (v17). The impermanence of life can bring clarity to how we live and what we are living for. Thus, what will you be remembered for?

Ole was a very frugal Norwegian, and so he had instructed his wife, Lena, that when he died that she shouldn't spend a lot of money. There was no need, for example, to put his picture in the paper or say lots of flowery things in an obituary. So when Ole died, Lena called the newspaper to place an obituary notice. "Just have it say, 'Ole died,'" she told the editor. "Well," the editor responded, "there is a minimum charge and you could certainly say more than just that." Lena thought for a moment, and then she said, "Well, then put this: 'Ole died. Ford pickup for sale.'"

When a summary statement is put in the newspaper for you, what will it say? How will you be remembered? In order to die well, we need to strive to leave a legacy that is beneficial to others.

One morning in 1888, Alfred Nobel opened the newspaper and read of his own passing. The alarming obituary notice was printed as a result of a journalistic error. It was, in fact, Alfred's brother Ludwig who had died, and a reporter carelessly attributed the death to the wrong Nobel family member. What Alfred read undoubtedly disturbed him deeply. The newspaper stated: "A man who can not very easily pass for a benefactor of humanity died yesterday in Cannes. It is Mr. Nobel, inventor of dynamite."

Many a preacher has embellished on or retold an apocryphal version of this story. The mistaken obituary is credited for turning Nobel's life around. It is claimed that he spent the rest of his life trying to establish a positive legacy as the result of it.

It is true that Alfred Nobel had been known for decades as "the dynamite king" and had amassed an extensive family fortune as the result. It is also undeniably true that the newspaper's judgment that Nobel could not be remembered as a benefactor to humanity would have been deeply disconcerting. It may, however, be folklore that it became the sole inspiration for his changed life. But by the end of his life he did become a positive benefactor to humanity. He bequeathed the bulk of his estate to be used as a fund to award those who "conferred the greatest benefit to humankind." Alfred Nobel is remembered today as the founder of the Nobel Peace Prize.

Sometimes people do not like the person they see staring back at them in the mirror and they decide they need to change. Certainly a contributing factor to that for Alfred Nobel was reading his own obituary. He is quoted as saying, "Every man ought to have the chance to correct his epitaph in midstream and write a new one." What would your obituary say if it appeared in the newspaper tomorrow? Are you satisfied with what your life will be remembered for?

A legacy is something that remains after we leave this world, something that speaks of our life. We desire that the world will be a better place because we have lived in it. Three concluding thoughts about leaving such a legacy:

Differentiate between Success and Significance

That is a concept I learned from Bob Buford's book entitled *Half Time*. It is a book about navigating a midlife crisis. In that book he very wisely spoke about the need to differentiate between success and significance.

Lakers legend Kobe Bryant, who tragically died the week I was writing this, is a picture of success. Kobe was a powerhouse on the basketball court with five championships, two Olympic gold medals and eighteen All-Star appearances. There are professional athletes who use their notoriety as a platform to accomplish significant things in life. But if at the end of life your only legacy is that you could put a round ball through a metal hoop better than the rest of humanity, that is not significant. Yes, you were prominent and popular, but that is not the same as significance.

Nurses who devote their life to caring for patients, teachers who invest their heart into their students, moms who sacrifice their own needs to shape the lives of their children, police officers who risk their lives in protecting others—that is significance. They leave an enduring mark on this world.

People who pursue success focus on how they can add value to themselves. People who pursue significance focus on how they can add value to others. A popular meme states, "Success is what happens *to* you, and significance is what happens *through* you."

> (Jesus said,) "When the Son of Man comes in his glory, and all the angels with him, he will sit on his glorious throne. All the nations will be gathered before him, and he will separate the people one from another as a shepherd separates the sheep from the goats. He will put the sheep on his right and the goats on his left" (Matthew 25:31-33).

All of humanity will fall into one of those two flocks.

> "Then the King will say to those on his right, 'Come, you who are blessed by my Father; take your inheritance, the kingdom prepared for you since the creation of the world. For I was hungry and you gave me something to eat, I was thirsty and you gave me something to drink, I was a stranger and you invited me in, I needed clothes and you clothed me, I was sick and you looked after me, I was in prison and you came to visit me.'

"Then the righteous will answer him,
'Lord, when did we see you hungry and
feed you, or thirsty and give you something to drink? When did we see you a
stranger and invite you in, or needing
clothes and clothe you? When did we
see you sick or in prison and go to
visit you?'

"The King will reply, 'Truly I tell you,
whatever you did for one of the least
of these brothers and sisters of mine,
you did for me' (Matthew 25:34-40).

Why is the passage so deliberately repetitious?
To drive home the point that it is the unacknowl-
edged acts of selfless service and the kindnesses
that rarely receive public acclaim that are in actu-
ality what is eternally significant. It is caring for the
ungrateful patient, it is love extended to the under-
achieving student, being patient with the rebellious
child, and giving to those who can never repay you.
Your face may not appear on the cover of *People
Magazine,* but your actions were significant. They
form a meaningful legacy.

That leads to a second and related thought associated with leaving a lasting legacy:

Live for a Cause, not for Applause

Solomon writes this about leaving a legacy:

"No one remembers the former generations, and even those yet to come will not be remembered by those who follow them" (Ecclesiastes 1:11).

You need to be mindful that in much of the book of Ecclesiastes, Solomon is writing from the perspective of the secular skeptic. He is meeting the unbelieving skeptic on their own ground. It's as if Solomon is saying, "Okay, let's look at life through the lens of secularism. Let's assume God is out of the picture. For the sake of discussion, God is irrelevant or nonexistent. But without God, is there any meaning or satisfaction to be found in life? I've been on that search, and this is where it led me. If you are striving to be remembered by future generations, well, forget that, because they will forget you! Future generations won't remember you no matter how important you are. You may get your 15 minutes of fame, but the spotlight invariably fades, and then what? So what?"

Author Max Lucado said simply, *"Outlive your life!"* We do that by leaving a legacy that has significance.

Solomon, playing the role of the secular skeptic would respond, "That's a bunch of hooey! You live, you die, no one remembers you. Meaningless, meaningless." You can hear his bitterness and cynicism and pessimism. Solomon is honestly reflecting the logical conclusion of a secular worldview.

But put God in the picture, and then we realize we are eternal spiritual beings. This life is but a short journey on the way to eternity. Therefore, we invest our life into what counts for eternity. Sure, it is tempting to seek the applause of an audience, but that will wane so quickly.

That leads to a closing application:

Get off your Butt

> "You can't make footprints in the sands of time if you're sitting on your butt. And who wants to make butt prints in the sands of time?"
> —Bob Moawad

Mr. Moawad, you are a master communicator! One could certainly choose a very memorable visual as a background for your statement.

In a clever and relevant twist on that phrase, Sean Stephenson wrote a book entitled *Get Off Your "But": How to End Self-Sabotage and Stand Up for Yourself.* Sean was born with brittle bones disease, a life-long genetic disorder. By the time he was 18 he had suffered 200 fractures. He reached an adult height of only three feet and is permanently confined to a wheelchair. Faced with an army of reasons to embrace self-pity, he chose instead to not succumb to the voices of negativity and excuse-making. He got off his excuse-making "Buts" and his booty. Sean graduated from college with high honors and has since inspired millions of people around the world through his motivational speaking and writing.

Henry Wadsworth Longfellow, in his poem "A Psalm of Life," reminds us of the potential inspiration a life well lived can provide to others:

> Lives of great men all remind us
> We can make our lives sublime,
> And, departing, leave behind us
> Footprints on the sands of time;

Footprints, that perhaps another,
Sailing o'er life's solemn main,
A forlorn and shipwrecked brother,
Seeing, shall take heart again.[15]

Everyone can benefit from an occasional foot to their fanny, a kick in the keister, a boot to their booty. But the motivating force in the life of a Christian should not be extrinsic but intrinsic. The motivational drive behind getting off our derriere in order to leave a positive legacy is the overflow of gratitude that we have because God has lavished his grace and mercy on us. Therefore, we desire to please him, and we long to hear him say, "Well done, good and faithful servant" (Matthew 25:21).

I conclude this chapter with a portion of a thought-provoking poem composed by C.T. Studd, missionary to China (1862–1931). Charles Thomas Studd was born into a family of wealth and privilege in England. After his brother became seriously ill, Charles was confronted by the question, "What is all the fame and flattery worth when a man comes to face eternity?" The poem he composed provides a fitting response to that question:

---

[15] Henry Wadsworth Longfellow, Ibid.

Two little lines I heard one day,
Traveling along life's busy way;
Bringing conviction to my heart,
And from my mind would not depart;
Only one life, 'twill soon be past,
Only what's done for Christ will last.
Only one life, yes only one,
Soon will its fleeting hours be done;
Then, in 'that day' my Lord to meet,
And stand before His Judgement seat;
Only one life, 'twill soon be past,
Only what's done for Christ will last...
Only one life, yes only one,
Now let me say, "Thy will be done";
And when at last I'll hear the call,
I know I'll say "twas worth it all";
Only one life, 'twill soon be past,
Only what's done for Christ will last. "[16]

Insight and Inspiration:

"The greatest legacy one can pass on
to one's children and grandchildren
is not money or other material things

---

[16] C.T. Studd, *Only One Life, Twill Soon Be Past.*

accumulated in one's life, but rather a legacy of character and faith."

—Billy Graham

"My mother was the most beautiful woman I ever saw. All I am I owe to my mother. I attribute my success in life to the moral, intellectual and physical education I received from her."

—George Washington

"All that I am or ever hope to be, I owe to my angel Mother."

—Abe Lincoln

"From my mother I learned the value of prayer, how to have dreams and believe I could make them come true."

—Ronald Reagan

"Let us endeavor so to live that when we come to die even the undertaker will be sorry."

—Mark Twain

Chapter 6

The Power of "I am"

Reflect upon this statement: "I am"—two of the most powerful words, for what you put after them shapes your reality.

That statement is referring to the importance of our self-definition. Sentences that begin with the words "I am" are statements about our identity. What we believe and say about ourselves has a significant impact on the outcome of our life. Therefore, life coaches and self-help gurus and mental health professionals are all trumpeting the importance of positive "I am" affirmations.

Throughout life, however, we have been through a conditioning process that has instilled an engrained mindset overflowing with "I am not" statements. "I am not smart. I am not talented. I am not...," and on and on the list goes. Those negative affirmations lead to self-defeating behaviors, interpersonal drama, and even acute or chronic illnesses.

Positive "I am" statements are helpful in rewriting the script of what we have been conditioned to believe about ourselves. Positive affirmations can be used to reprogram the subconscious mind by replacing those negative and counterproductive beliefs. I use this statement frequently in counseling sessions: "Our beliefs inform our emotions; our *emotions* put us *in motion* and produce a behavior. Change your thoughts to change your life."

A needed word of caution—bookstores and blogs overflow with unhelpful "I am" instruction that may be a mixture of pop psychology, prosperity gospel theology, and even pantheistic ideology. "I am" affirmations need to be grounded in truth. There is, therefore, wisdom and value in "I am" affirmations that reflect the truth found in Scripture.

There is an "I am" statement taken from a song title that is very relevant to the theme of this book. The statement has the power to transform how we plan to live and how we prepare to die. The affirmation and the song title is "I am a Wayfaring Stranger."

The song, like many traditional folk songs, is of uncertain origin. Some trace its origin to Appalachian folk music, others believe it has older Irish roots, and some speculate that its origin rests in the spirituals that slaves sang.

During and for several years after the Civil War, the song was known as the "Libby Prison Hymn." The reason for that was the words had been inscribed by a dying Union soldier on a wall in Libby Prison, a Confederate prison that had gained an infamous reputation for its overcrowded and harsh conditions. It was believed that the dying soldier had authored the song to comfort another soldier, but since the song had been published several years before the Civil War began, that was clearly not the case. That story, however, reveals the comfort that flows from embracing our identity as a wayfarer through this world. A comfort that comes from knowing we will be released from the prison of pain in this life and that heaven awaits us. The song tells of the hardships and struggles of our journey through this world and then of our hope of being reunited with loved ones in heaven when we die.

> *Wayfaring Stranger*
> I am a poor wayfaring stranger,
> I'm trav'ling through this world of woe;
> There is no sickness, toil, or danger,
> In that bright world to which I go.
> I'm going there to see my father,
> I'm going there no more to roam;
> I'm just a going over Jordan,
> I'm just a going over home.
> I know dark clouds will gather round me,
> I know my pathway's rough and steep;
> But golden fields lie out before me,
> Where weary eyes no more shall weep.
> I'm going there to see my mother,
> She said she'd meet me when I come;
> I'm just a going over Jordan,
> I'm just a going over home.
> I want to sing salvation's story,
> In concert with the blood-washed band;
> I want to wear a crown of glory,
> When I get home to that good land.
> I'm going there to see my brothers,
> They passed before me one by one;
> I'm just a going over Jordan,

I'm just a going over home.
I'll soon be free from every trial,
This form will rest beneath the sod;
I'll drop the cross of self-denial,
And enter in my home with God.
I'm going there to see my Savior,
Who shed for me His precious blood;
I'm just a going over Jordan,
I'm just a going over home.

The song is written in a mournful sounding minor key, but it is a song of joyful anticipation. Consider the words in the title for a moment. A wayfarer is a traveler, especially one who travels by foot. (As we travel through this life, we leave our footprints on the sands of time. There is our tie-in to the last chapter about leaving a legacy.) The word *Stranger* in the song title is a repeated biblical theme. It is found, for example, in Hebrews 11, a chapter that is referred to as "Faith's Hall of Fame" because it recounts the faith of many Old Testament figures.

> All these people were still living by faith when they died. They did not receive the things promised; they only saw them and welcomed them from a distance, admitting that they were

foreigners and strangers on earth... they were longing for a better country—a heavenly one. Therefore, God is not ashamed to be called their God, for he has prepared a city for them (Hebrews 11:13,16).

Why were they called foreigners and strangers on earth? Because this world is not our home. We are children of God, and we are away from our heavenly Father. Our citizenship is in heaven.

If we internalize our identity as a wayfarer, it will change our perspective on how to live. We will live more purposefully and intentionally because of the clarity that the affirmation brings. How so? Let me suggest three very broad applications by completing this sentence: "I am a wayfaring stranger, therefore, I will...

live more fully present in the moment."

In 2004, Tim McGraw's song "Live Like You Were Dyin'" was voted the number one country song of the year by Billboard Year-End. The song lyrics recount a conversation between two people. A man in his early 40s had just received an unexpected and terminal medical diagnosis. As he processed his options and the precious time he might have remaining, he was asked, "How's it hit you, when you get that kind of news and what did you do?"

His response to that question is heard in the chorus. The dying man chose to engage in adventurous and adrenaline-pumping activities such as sky-diving and bull riding. But he also embraced the relational aspects of life by loving deeper and reconciling relationships through forgiveness. Those positive changes in life then prompted the dying man to wish that everyone would get the chance to live as if they were dying.[17]

News flash: We are all dying. This is our chance! So why don't we live as if we are dying? What would that look like? How does someone who truly believes they are a wayfaring stranger live?

McGraw's song provides a good starting point for an answer. We would live more joyfully and fully present in the moment, and we would cherish our relationships more.

---

[17] "Live Like You Were Dying" was the title track on Tim McGraw's eighth album. The album was certified 4 x Platinum and was nominated for two Grammys in 2005, winning for Best Male Country Vocal Performance.

That's not exactly the answer you get from a fundamentalist preacher. They preach that we are pilgrims passing through and, therefore, we need to live separate from this evil world. We need to live more sober-mindedly, we need to suffer for Jesus, and we need to look as if we have sucked on lemons. (And we wonder why non-Christians find the "Christian" life so unappealing.)

Hunter Thompson provided this sage advice, "Life should not be a journey to the grave with the intention of arriving safely in a pretty and well preserved body, but rather to skid in broadside in a cloud of smoke, thoroughly used up, totally worn out, and loudly proclaiming 'Wow! What a Ride!'"[18]

"I am a wayfaring stranger, therefore, I will...

hold onto earthly treasures loosely."

(Jesus said,) "'Do not store up for yourselves treasures on earth,...But store up for yourselves treasures in heaven, ...For where your treasure is, there your heart will be also'" (Matthew 6:19,21).

---

[18] Hunter S. Thompson, *The Proud Highway: Sage of a Desperate Southern Gentleman*, 1955–1967.

Randy Alcorn, reflecting upon those words, writes, "He who lays up treasures on earth spends his life backing away from his treasures. To him, death is loss. He who lays up treasures in heaven looks forward to eternity; he's moving daily toward his treasures. To him, death is gain. He who spends his life moving toward his treasures has reason to rejoice. Are you despairing or rejoicing?"[19]

C.S. Lewis continues with the same line of questioning. He wonders, "Has this world been so kind to you that you should leave it with regret? There are better things ahead than any we leave behind."[20]

The differentiation between death as loss or gain in Alcorn's statement and the "better things ahead" in Lewis's statement are reminiscent of Paul's words:

> For to me, living means living for Christ, and dying is even better. But if I live, I can do more fruitful work for Christ. So I really don't know which is better. I'm torn between two desires: I long to go and be with Christ, which

---

[19] Randy Alcorn, *The Treasure Principle: Discovering the Secret of Joyful Giving*, (Multnomah, 2012), 49.

[20] C. S. Lewis, *Letters to an American Lady*, (Wm. B. Eerdmans Publishing), 124.

would be far better for me (Philippians 1:21-23; NLT).

If we try to cling onto earthly treasures, our lives will be marked by despair and regret. One never sees a U-Haul at a funeral. Joy and freedom come from embracing our identity as a wayfaring stranger passing through this world. The fact that we don't view death with a greater sense of peace in our soul just might be because we think of death as taking us *from* our treasures rather than bringing us *to* the treasure of heaven.

"I am a wayfaring stranger, therefore, I will...

invest my life in what has eternal significance."

Arthur Miller's play *Death of a Salesman* illustrates very poignantly the connection between identity and the resulting course in life that one pursues. Willy Loman, the main character, is an aging traveling salesman with a declining career. The play chronicles his self-destruction as his life crumbles around him. To cope, Willy retreats into a delusional world of how popular, influential, and successful he believes himself to be. Tragically, he imposes his shallow values and aspirations on his two sons.

The emotional lynchpin of the play is the conflicted relationship between Willy and his older, less successful son, Biff, who had grown to resent his father for insisting he pursue a life he didn't want.

Devastated and desperate, Willy ends his own life. The final scene in the play takes place at his graveside where Biff declares that Willy "had the wrong dreams" and that "he never knew who he was." Those phrases reveal the play's message—if someone lacks an accurate sense of identity, they will spend their life pursuing the wrong goals.

Do you know who you are? Is who you are determined by what you do, or is what you do determined by who you are? Willy subscribed to the first view. A follower of Jesus subscribes to the latter.

The words we place after "I am" will indeed shape the course of our life. Our hope for meaning and fulfillment is based on the critical foundation of our beliefs regarding who we are. Our willingness to embrace our identity as a wayfaring stranger passing through this world of woe, our willingness to accept eternity as our dominant reality, and our ability to weigh life's various options on the scale of eternity is what we call an *eternal perspective*.

An eternal perspective runs counter to the Epicurean-like philosophy that is so prevalent in our society. Such self-oriented hedonism never satisfies the longing of our soul. We were created for so much more than the shallow objective of eat, drink, and be merry. This life was meant to be lived in light of the one to come.

Inspiration and Insight:

"I am a wayfaring stranger; therefore, I will live more fully present in the moment."

Compare and contrast these two statements:

> "Life is not measured by how many breaths we take, but by the moments that take our breath away."
> —Maya Angelou

> "We are not meant to embrace moments, but to embrace God. Moments are not always good; God is never anything else but good. Moments are simply the place where we meet him."
> —John Ortberg, *God is Closer than You Think*

"I am a wayfaring stranger; therefore, I will hold onto earthly treasures loosely."

> Were the whole realm of nature mine,
> That were a present far too small;
> Love so amazing, so divine,
> Demands my soul, my life, my all.
>
> —Isaac Watts

"I am a wayfaring stranger; therefore, I will invest my life in what has eternal significance."

> "I am willing that my house on earth be emptier (if only) His house be fuller."
> —Jim Elliot, martyred missionary

> Some want to live within the sound
> Of church or chapel bell;
> I want to run a rescue shop,
> Within a yard of hell.
> —C.T. Studd

Chapter 7

Facing the Final Curtain

I n Solomon's search for meaning and purpose and
satisfaction in life, he comes to this conclusion:

> Better to spend your time at funerals
> than at parties.
> After all, everyone dies—
> so the living should take this to heart.
> Sorrow is better than laughter,
> for sadness has a refining influence on
> us (Ecclesiastes 7:2–3; NLT).

The parallelism in the sentence structure explains
Solomon's intent. Funerals and sorrow are better
than parties and laughter. Why is that? Because we
grow reflective, and our character may be refined;
we become introspective, and we may gain insight
through the emotion of sadness and through the

experience of attending funerals. The living should take this to heart.

In this chapter we will be attending a funeral. There are two funerals in the closing chapters of Genesis, first for Jacob and then for Joseph. It is, by the way, an instructive insight to note that the book of Genesis begins with the statement, "In the beginning God created (life)...," and the concluding words recorded in Genesis are, "Joseph was placed in a coffin in Egypt." The book ends with that phrase! Genesis moves from creation of life to a coffin. Something has gone terribly wrong!

We pick up the story line of Jacob's funeral at the end of chapter 47.

> Jacob lived in Egypt seventeen years, and the years of his life were a hundred and forty-seven. When the time drew near for Israel [i.e., Jacob] to die, he called for his son Joseph and said to him, "If I have found favor in your eyes, put your hand under my thigh and promise that you will show me kindness and faithfulness. Do not bury me in Egypt, but when I rest

with my fathers, carry me out of Egypt
and bury me where they are buried."
(Genesis 47:28-30)

"When the time drew near for Israel to die...," that
is a striking phrase, is it not? Anyone reading the
text with any thought realizes that one day his or
her name will be inserted into that sentence as well.
Irrespective of how health conscious you might be,
that final exit sign on the highway of life will even-
tually appear. It is said that a healthy lifestyle is just
a phrase used to describe a slower rate of dying.
There will come a day when it will be apparent
that the time has drawn near for us to face the
final curtain.

Frank Sinatra is remembered for his song "My
Way," which contains that phrase. It is a popular
song choice at funeral services. The lyrics, however, reflect a bit of a dismissive and defiant stance
before the curtain of death. The singer boastfully
proclaims that as the end draws near and they
face the final curtain, they do life their way. On one
occasion, Sinatra collapsed on stage while singing
that very song. They had to bring a wheelchair, put
him in the chair, and then wheel him off stage. One

would think there might have been some flash of insight at that moment.[21]

We can't ignore the inevitable. We will all face the final curtain, but as a society we have attempted to anesthetize ourselves from that inescapable event. For most of the last century, death has moved steadily away from our view. Death has moved from the home to the hospital. In 1908, only 14 percent of all deaths occurred in an institutional setting, either a hospital, nursing home, or other such facility. Currently, that figure is somewhere between 75 and 80 percent. The dying are being pushed out of sight. It is not unusual for someone in our society to be beyond middle age before they have their first intimate encounter with someone dying.[22]

We live in a time when advanced medicine wards off death, but it doesn't prepare us for peaceful ones. Death, however, is not just a medical battle to be fought. Death is not just the loss of precious relationships, which we then grieve over. Death is a spiritual event that requires forethought and

---

[21] Alistar Begg's teaching on Truth for Life provides inspiration for this chapter. In particular his message *Famous Last Words* (12/15/1996) and *Leaving a Legacy* (2/21/2019).

[22] Rob Moll, *The Art of Dying*, (Downers Grove, IL. InterVarsity Press, 2010), pp. 15–16.

preparation. Therefore, it is better to spend your time at funerals than parties.

"When the time drew near for Israel to die"; when the time draws near for you to die, the question you must answer is, "Am I prepared to die?" And indeed, no pastor has done his job properly, nor prepared his people effectively to live life in all its fullness, unless he has prepared them to meet death and to make that final passing journey.

Jacob serves as a wonderful illustration of preparing to die. First of all, he faced the fact that he was going to die. He didn't know the exact time, but he had a sense that he probably shouldn't, as they say, be buying green bananas. His shelf life was nearing its end. He is aware that he has gone into extra innings. He is well beyond the ninth inning; the game will soon be over.

Bette Davis nailed it when she said, "Old age ain't no place for sissies." Jacob, at 147 years old, undoubtedly would have agreed.

Notice that Jacob had a heightened level of concern about putting his affairs in order. He called for his son Joseph and said to him, "If I have found favor in your eyes, put your hand under my thigh and promise that you will show me kindness and faithfulness" (v29).

What was that all about? It was a symbolic gesture, a custom at that time associated with making a pledge or an oath. "Joseph, promise me this." And Joseph undoubtedly said, "You've got it, Dad. What do you want?" And then Jacob said, "Do not bury me in Egypt, but when I rest with my fathers, carry me out of Egypt and bury me where they are buried."

There is a lesson here in how to prepare adequately for your own funeral. Have you made arrangements? Have you discussed funeral plans with your mate or your children? Do they know what you desire in that regard? I have sat with families on numerous occasions and tried to navigate them through the funeral-planning process because mom didn't make her wishes known. And as her adult children are fighting in front of me, I'm quite sure that mom's wishes would have been that they didn't fight!

Jacob's concern for the location of his burial is not primarily about geography; it is about the testimony of faith that he wants to leave with his children and grandchildren. Jacob recognized that in his death, he could make a statement about God's unfolding plan of his covenant relationship with his people. God had promised Jacob's grandpa Abraham that he would become the father of a great nation and that he would give his descendants a land. That promise passed through his son Isaac and then into the life of Jacob. And so, as Jacob draws near to the end of his days, he wants to ensure that those who follow after him would be absolutely clear about that.

In the movie *Fiddler on the Roof* when Tevye sings about tradition, he stops ever so often to make statements regarding tradition. We remember the line, "Without tradition we would be as shaky as a fiddler on the roof." At another point Tevye says, "Tradition teaches us who we are and what God expects of us."

"Tradition teaches us *who we are*." (Flashback to chapter 6.) Jacob wants to remind his sons and his grandchildren about who they are. They are God's chosen people and the recipients of a promise. God would bring them into a land he promised to them. Jacob expresses his faith in that promise by wanting to be buried in the Promised Land.

The essential questions of life become: "Who am I?" and "Where do I go when I die?" And to that, Jacob stands as a classic witness. He was declaring his faith in the certainty of God's promise to his children.

I'll summarize the closing chapters of Genesis: In chapter 48, Jacob pronounces a blessing upon his grandsons, Joseph's two sons. Chapter 49 records Jacob's blessing and prophetic word over each of his 12 sons. He then repeats his instruction regarding his burial in front of all of them, which again, was a testimony of his faith in God. And then that chapter ends with this statement:

> When Jacob had finished giving instruc-
> tions to his sons, he drew his feet up
> into the bed, breathed his last and was
> gathered to his people (Genesis 49:33).

That is a picture of dying well. Your family is gathered. You give them assurance of your faith. You bless them. And then you pass from this life into God's presence.

Do you know who you are? From that moment of salvation when we were spiritually born again, we became God's children. We are now wayfaring strangers away from our heavenly Father looking forward to our home in heaven with him. What kind of statement of faith do you want to make through your death and through your funeral?

In 125 AD, Aristides, a pagan Greek, wrote to a friend about the extraordinary appeal of Christianity that resulted from the response Christians displayed at death. A sentence from one of his letters reads, "If any righteous man among the Christians passes from this world, they rejoice and offer thanks to God, and they escort the body with songs and thanksgiving as if he were setting out from one place to another nearby."

And so it is! At death, believers set out from one place to another. There is reason for sorrow but not as those who "grieve without hope."

John Chrysostom, one of the early Church fathers, summarized the Christian's attitude toward death when he wrote:

> When a dear one dies, the unbeliever
> sees a cadaver, but the Christian sees a
> body asleep. The unbeliever says that
> the dead person has "gone." We agree,

but we remember where he has gone.
He has gone where the apostle Paul is,
where Peter is, where the whole company of the saints are. We remember
that he will rise, not with tears of
dismay, but with splendor and glory.

There should be, for us as followers of Jesus, in
our approach to death certain things that leave
no doubt in the minds of the watching world. We
understand that death is to be with Christ, which
is better by far. Death is to be reunited with all our
loved ones who knew Jesus as their Savior.

Questions about whether one should be cremated
or whether we get buried in a box are not really the
issue. I don't believe you will find any prescriptive
way of disposing of the body in the Bible. There
may be sentimental reasons or emotional reasons
to be laid to rest in a family burial plot, but it doesn't
really matter.

Can I ask you two questions? If you died tonight,
would you go to heaven? And secondly, how do
you know that you won't die tonight? Now if your
answer is anything less than yes to question one,
and since no one can answer question two with

certitude, are you prepared to take a chance? Okay, that's three questions. But the hope of your eternal destiny is based on something, so would it not make sense to base your hope on the only One who has walked through death and come out on the other side? Would it not make sense to base your hope on the One who said, "I am the resurrection and the life. The one who believes in me will live, even though they die."

The Book of Life

There was a man by the name of James Milton Black who composed a hymn back in 1893. The inspiration for the hymn flowed from an occasion when a girl was absent from his Sunday school class. He had met this girl as he was passing through an alley one day. She was a tattered fourteen-year-old, the daughter of an alcoholic. His heart was drawn to her, and he invited her to his class and youth group, which she began to attend. One day when he took roll, the girl was absent. He sensed something eerie in the silence after he called her name. Later that day, he went to the girl's home to check on her. He found her seriously ill and sent for his own doctor. The doctor said that she had pneumonia and that death was imminent.

Deeply moved by that news, James returned home and sat at his piano. He tried to find a song to fit the thought of a heavenly roll call, but he could not locate one. He felt prompted to compose the song we now know by the title "When the Roll Is Called up Yonder." Tragically, only a few days later, he had the sad opportunity of explaining how he came to write the song when he performed it at the funeral of the girl whose absence at roll call had inspired it.

> When the trumpet of the Lord shall sound,
> And time will be no more,
> And the morning breaks, eternal, bright and fair;
> When the saved of earth shall gather
> Over on the other shore,
> And the roll is called up yonder,
> I'll be there!
> On that bright and cloudless morning
> when the dead in Christ shall rise,
> and the glory of his resurrection share;
> when his chosen ones shall gather
> to their home beyond the skies,
> and the roll is called up yonder,
> I'll be there.

There is a roll. It's called the Lamb's book of life. Either your name is written in that book or your name is not in it. So heed this warning:

"Anyone whose name was not found written in the book of life was thrown into the lake of fire" (Revelation 20:15).

It absolutely is better to spend your time at funerals than at parties if it causes you to prepare for eternity.

Insight and Inspiration:

Edmund Gwenn observed, "Dying is easy. Comedy is difficult." Any comedian will tell you, comedy about dying is very hard. Perhaps it is necessary and needed though. Necessary to lighten the mood; needed to cause us to ponder life and death. Here's an attempt to lighten the mood:

> "I've had so much plastic surgery that when I die, they'll donate my body to Tupperware."
> —Joan Rivers

> "They say such nice things about people at their funerals that it makes me sad

that I'm going to miss mine by just a few days."
                              —Garrison Keillor

The epitaph comedian Rodney Dangerfield chose for his memorial stone reads: "There goes the neighborhood."

When George Burns was in his late 90s, he was asked if his doctor knew he still smoked. Burns responded, "No...he's dead."

Chapter 8

Finishing Well

> "I have fought the good fight, I have finished the race,..." (2 Timothy 4:7).

That statement is one of the most frequently selected verses to be placed in the funeral memorial card or to have read during the funeral service. All too often, however, that verse wasn't chosen because the deceased was devoted to the cause of Christ. The selection of that text was not prompted by their dedication to some ministry-serving position in their church. The passage was chosen by family members because their loved one had tried every medical option to stay alive. They had endured numerous and painful surgeries in valiant attempts by doctors to prolong their life. They had fought desperately to stay alive.

Christian physician John Dunlop, who teaches end-of-life ethics at Trinity Evangelical Divinity School, speaks directly to this issue. "I view the practice of medicine as part of our taking dominion over the earth...It's good. But not when we're shaking our fist in God's face and saying, 'No, I'm not going to die yet. I'm trusting technology to pull me through.'"[23]

We could have a discussion at this point about the ethics of prolonging life through medical intervention. Are we prolonging life? Or are we prolonging suffering? We could debate the morality of allowing life to end. Are we playing God with that decision? Or do we lack faith that God could heal?

Some of us have wrestled with those heart-wrenching questions and decisions when a loved one is gravely ill. We know how hurtful a glib or a dogmatic answer can be. In contemplating those dilemmas, we can find guidance from the insight Paul provides in his response to the end of his own life.

> ...the time for my departure is near. I have fought the good fight, I have

---

[23] Rob Moll, *The Art of Dying,* (Downers Grove, IL. InterVarsity Press, 2010), p. 38.

finished the race, I have kept the faith. Now there is in store for me the crown of righteousness, which the Lord, the righteous Judge, will award to me on that day—and not only to me, but also to all who have longed for his appearing (2 Timothy 4:6–8).

When Paul wrote those words, he was in a dismal underground dungeon known as the Mamertine Prison. It was a maximum-security prison for Rome's chief enemies. Tradition says Peter was also imprisoned there at some point in time. Today a white structure has been built above the dungeon, and it is a place of Christian worship.

Thus, Paul was in chains when these words were written to Timothy. The preliminary hearing of his case had already taken place. He was awaiting the full trial, but he was not expecting to be acquitted. He was very aware that the executioner's sword lay in his near future. He writes this letter with a passionate concern to ensure that the Good News of Jesus would be guarded and then passed on to subsequent generations.

English writer Samuel Johnson said, "When a man knows he is to be hanged in a fortnight, it concentrates his mind wonderfully."

So true! There is nothing like impending death to clarify and prioritize the issues of life. Paul knew that in all likelihood he was writing what would essentially be his last will and testament to the Church. This is his final letter, his final chapter. Facing the prospect of death, he writes this letter, his swan song, his last words to Timothy to whom he is passing the baton of faith.

Verse 6 in a translation known as the Message reads like this: "You take over. I'm about to die." What is striking is how matter-of-fact that statement is. "I'm about to die. What's for breakfast? It looks like rain today." There is no indication of terror in his words.

Attitudes toward death fluctuate across an emotional continuum. On one end of the spectrum is the rage heard in the poem "Do Not Go Gentle into That Good Night," composed by Welsh poet Dylan Thomas. The narrator of the poem is urging their father to struggle against his decline in health and impending death—*"Rage against the dying of the light."*

Attitudes toward death range from that to gentle acceptance and peaceful resolve. There is acceptance in Paul's words. "I'm about to die," (MSG) "the time for my departure is near" (NIV).

Why such serenity? Part of the explanation as to why Paul didn't experience an undue amount of anxiety is found in the term "departure." In the original language the word is *analusis*, from the verb "to loosen." There were several usages of that word that linked it with dying, various connotations that have brought peace to the followers of Jesus throughout the ages.

A Collapsing Tent

It was a word used of a soldier loosening the ropes when taking down a tent. That would have been a familiar picture for Paul, who was a tent maker by trade. We see him use that metaphor in his writing.

> For we know that when this earthly tent we live in is taken down (that is, when we die and leave this earthly body), we will have a house in heaven, an eternal body made for us by God himself and not by human hands. We grow weary

in our present bodies, and we long to put on our heavenly bodies like new clothing (2 Corinthians 5:1–2).

"Strike the tent," were the final words of General Robert E. Lee when he died. It is a biblical word picture of death. Strike the tent and move on from this battlefield.

A nonbeliever generally approaches death with trepidation for the same reason that someone cautiously goes through a door into a dark room. They don't know what is on the other side of that door. That room might hold a psychopathic killer, or it may contain furniture they will stub their toes on. Paul, by way of contrast, was absolutely confident of what lay beyond death's door.

A Sailing Ship

The word "departure" was also used of untying a boat from its moorings. That is a beautiful picture of dying. Loosen the mooring lines, weigh anchor, and sail from the storm-tossed seas of this life for the safe harbor of heaven. That word picture inspired a poem entitled "Gone from Sight." The poem is used in hospice literature and has brought comfort to countless numbers of people.

"Gone from Sight"

I am standing upon the seashore.
A ship, at my side,
spreads her white sails to the moving
breeze and starts for the blue ocean.
She is an object of beauty and strength.
I stand and watch her until; at length,
she hangs like a speck of white cloud
just where the sea and sky come to
mingle with each other.

Then, someone at my side says, "There,
she is gone."

Gone where?

Gone from my sight. That is all. She is
just as large in mast,
hull and spar as she was when she
left my side.

And, she is just as able to bear her load
of living freight to her destined port.

Her diminished size is in me—not in her.

And, just at the moment when someone says, "There, she is gone," there are other eyes watching her coming, and other voices ready to take up the glad shout, "Here she comes!"

And that is dying.

That poem is sometimes known as "The Parable of Immortality." The soul, the essential part of who we are, is immortal. For the Christian, that means the soul departs from the seas of this life and is then greeted by those who have already departed.

I imagine Paul would have found a connection and comfort in this word picture also. He had sailed across the mercurial waters of the Mediterranean several times. And now, soon his soul would weigh anchor from his body and set sail for the safe harbor of heaven. The old Gospel tune "One Day My Ship Will Sail" is based upon this word picture.

A Loosened Yoke

There is a third word picture associated with the term *departure.* The word was also used of loosening oxen from the yoke on their neck. The farmer would take the harness off the animal at the close of the workday, give it a swat on the rump, and send it out into the pasture to rest. Paul had borne that yoke of ministry for many years.

My departure is near. This is the same word that is used in the Philippians' passage that I have already referenced in this book.

> For to me, to live is Christ and to die is gain. If I am to go on living in the body, this will mean fruitful labor for me. Yet what shall I choose? I do not know! I am torn between the two: I desire to depart [*i.e., to have the yoke loosened and lifted from my shoulders*] and be with Christ, which is better by far (Philippians 1:21–23; all emphasis added).

"to depart and be with Christ"—No time lag, no waiting room, no soul sleep. When I die, I will be

immediately ushered into the presence of God. "Rage, rage against the dying of the light"; No way! To depart and be with Christ is better by far. Paul was enthralled with the prospect of heaven.

Back to our 1st Timothy text—I have fought the good fight, I have finished the race, I have kept the faith (4:7).

In the Greek text the nouns come first in each phrase, so it actually reads like this: The fight, I have fought. The race, I have finished. The faith, I have kept. The words *fight* and *fought* come from the same Greek word. It is the root word *agon* from which our English word agony is derived. "I have struggled the good struggle" would be a fitting paraphrase. "I have given the contest my total effort. I finished well."

Finishing Well

Richard Cumberland, an English theologian and Anglican bishop during the 1600s, is credited with the statement, "It's better to wear out than rust out." We have all heard that statement, but I find it noteworthy that it was originally used in the context of contending for the Christian faith.

*It's better to wear out...*from fighting the good fight and running all the way to the finish line... *than rust out.*

We are inclined to think that the greatest resource of a local church is in its youth. The future of the Church is of course, in its youth, but a church's resource is not in its youth. Youth don't have the experience or the wisdom that comes from years of living the Christian life. Nor do young adults have the time with the demands of raising their families. The real resource of a church lies in the people who are over the age of 66. But just at the point when people have put themselves into a position, financially and emotionally and spiritually, to become an incredible resource; they start to talk about fossilizing in Florida or aging away in Arizona. Then they disappear and rust away.

Ralph Winter, the founder of the Center for World Missions, wrote an article entitled "The Retirement Booby Trap." In it he said, "Most men don't die of old age; they die of retirement." He was still traveling, speaking, and writing for the cause of world missions until he departed from this life at age 84.

What are you planning to do after the age of 66? Resist the typical American dream of retirement. Resolve to live out your retirement years with a greater purpose in mind than to chase a golf ball on the fairway. Don't just wait out the clock until you die. Don't sit on the resource. Dying well means living with passion and purpose right up to the moment that death arrives.

God created us to engage in productive work. The Garden of Eden wasn't a place where Adam laid in a hammock and drank tree of life smoothies. God planted a garden and instructed Adam to cultivate it and keep it.

In verse 8 we hear another reason why Paul didn't display an anxious dread over his impending death.

> Now there is in store for me the crown of righteousness, which the Lord, the righteous Judge, will award to me on that day—and not only to me, but also to all who have longed for his appearing (4:8).

Comedian George Carlin cynically said, "Life is tough, then you die!" Paul says, "Life is tough, but the future is glorious! The future for me holds the crown of righteousness."

Note again the language of certainty. There is no doubt or lack of conviction in what Paul believes. This is not, "I hope that somehow or another, this will be the outcome." No, he says, "It is laid up for me and not only for me but to all who fight the good fight, and run to the finish line, and keep the faith."

Inspiration and Insight:

> "*Golden years* must have been coined by the young. It is doubtful that anyone over seventy would have described this phase of life with such a symbolic word. Perhaps a compassionate soul kindly slipped a *g* in front of the word *old* to ease the ache of reality."
>
> —Billy Graham, in his book *Nearing Home: Life, Faith, and Finishing Well*. Rev. Graham wrote the book when he was in his 90s.[24]

---

[24] Billy Graham, *Nearing Home—Life, Faith, and Finishing Well,* (Thomas Nelson, Nashville, TN, 2011), p. 51.

"Many people die at twenty-five and aren't buried until they are seventy-five."
—Benjamin Franklin

"As a well-spent day brings a happy sleep, so a well-employed life brings a happy death."
—Leonardo Da Vinci

"I press on toward the goal to win the prize for which God has called me heavenward in Christ Jesus."
—Paul in Philippians 3:14

Chapter 9

Going Home

T homas Dorsey was a Black jazz musician originally from Georgia. In the 1920s he gained a certain amount of notoriety as the composer of jazz tunes with suggestive lyrics. He performed regularly in Al Capone's speakeasies and other after-hour spots in Chicago, where he gained the nickname "the Whispering Piano Player." That was during the era of the Prohibition, and Dorsey performed quietly enough to avoid drawing police attention.

At the age of twenty-one, his hectic and unhealthy lifestyle led to a nervous breakdown. Tom convalesced back home in Atlanta. There his mother admonished him to stop playing the blues and to serve the Lord. He ignored her advice and returned to Chicago, but a second breakdown left him unable to play music. After his recovery this time, Dorsey returned to the Christian upbringing instilled in him by his parents, and he committed himself to composing spiritual music. He combined the syncopated notes of a twelve-bar blues structure to spiritual lyrics. His music helped usher in what is known as the golden age of gospel music.

Thomas Dorsey is known today as the father of gospel music. He composed over 400 songs; one of his best known works is "Peace in the Valley." He also wrote "Precious Lord, Take my Hand." The background story to that song gives us insight for those times when we are in life's dark valleys.

The year was 1932, and times were hard for Dorsey. Times were hard for everyone. That was the peak unemployment year during the Great Depression when the jobless figure hovered around 25 percent. Tens of thousands were traveling the roads and rails looking for work. Trying to survive the Depression years was an especially difficult proposition for a musician. On top of that, Dorsey's music was not accepted by many pastors. Some said it was much too worldly—"the devil's music," they called it. Years later Dorsey could laugh about it. He said,

"I got kicked out of some of the best churches in the land."

One night in St. Louis, Dorsey received a telegram informing him that his wife Nettie died while giving birth to their son. The child died shortly thereafter. Dorsey was filled with grief, and his faith was shaken. In the midst of that dark valley, he turned to what he knew best—music. He composed the song "Precious Lord, Take my Hand."

> Precious Lord, take my hand
> Lead me on, help me stand
> I'm tired, I am weak, and I'm worn
> Through the storm, through the night
> Lead me on to the light
> Precious Lord, take my hand and
> lead me home.

There is an important word in those lyrics that we need to note. It's the word *through*. "Through the storm, through the night...," as in Psalm 23—"Even though I walk *through* the darkest valley." Some people get stuck *in* the valley but there is a *through* the valley. When we rely upon the Shepherd, he will lead us not just *to* the valley but *through* the valley.

The comforting phrase that has endeared the song to so many is the plea that each verse ends with *"Precious Lord, take my hand and lead me home."* That longing for home so resonates with people that Dorsey's song has been translated into over fifty languages.

Why do we long for home? There is a saying, "Home is where your story begins." We long for home because home is the place where we are supposed to belong. That is one of the basic psychological needs all people have—the need to belong.

Home is supposed to be a place where you are welcomed and accepted and loved and celebrated and honored and you belong just because you are you and you are home. We have all kinds of language around that. We speak about being the "home-town boy" or having a "home field advantage" just because we are home. To varying degrees, we sensed that in the home where our story began.[25]

There is another saying; "Home is where your heart is." The concepts of home and heart can never be

---

[25] I'm indebted to the writing of John Ortberg from a number of sources for his thoughts on home. John Ortberg, *Everybody's Normal Till You Get to Know Them,* (Grand Rapid, MI. Zondervan, 2003), p. 225.

completely separated. The Pew Research Center conducted a survey of 2,260 American adults; among other things, they asked participants to identify "the place in your heart you consider to be home."

How would you have responded? Only 22 percent of the respondents identified the place they were currently living to be home. Twenty-six percent of the respondents reported that home was where they were born or raised. Eighteen percent identified home as the place that they had lived the longest. Fifteen percent felt that it was where their family had come from, and four percent said that home was where they had gone to high school.

There is a longing inside of the human heart for home, but the truth is no home in this fallen world will ever completely satisfy that longing. That is why there isn't agreement on where home is. That is why we can speak of broken homes and dysfunctional homes, yet we also talk about being homesick. Behind that longing for home is the yearning cry of our soul for God and to be reunited with our Creator.

Our Home in Heaven

In one of the most comforting passages in the entire Bible, Jesus promised a home in heaven. Let's walk through that promise.

(Jesus said,) "Do not let your hearts be troubled. You believe in God; believe also in me" (John 14:1).

Troubled—the word means to be disturbed or agitated. Jesus uses the word metaphorically of the disciples' emotional reaction to his announcement of his imminent death. Imagine a tranquil lake surface that is turned tumultuous by a sudden raging storm. The disciples were experiencing such an emotional storm-tossed and troubled sea.

Jesus also knew what it was to be troubled. The same Greek word is used to describe emotions he experienced. He said, "My soul is troubled" when he thought about being crucified (John 12:27). We also read that Jesus was deeply troubled when he told his disciples that one of them was going to betray him (John 13:21).

Jesus is, therefore, not telling the disciples to deny or suppress their emotions. God created us emotional beings. Emotions are not good or bad, right or wrong. Emotions are messengers from the front line. What Jesus is trying to teach the disciples is that life does not have to be controlled by our emotional reaction to outward circumstances. Our beliefs inform our emotions, our *emotions* put us *in-motion* and produce a behavior. We can change our emotional state and our ensuing behaviors by shifting the focus of what is consuming our thoughts.

What then should we focus our minds on during troubling periods of grief? Jesus instructs the disciples to redirect their thoughts to who they knew.

"Do not let your hearts be troubled. You believe in God; believe also in me" (John 14:1).

He is saying, "Remind yourself of what you know about me. You've lived with me for three years. You have learned from me and about me. Fix your thoughts on me."

Then Jesus instructs the disciples to redirect their thoughts to where they will go, their destination after death.

"There is more than enough room in my Father's home. If this were not so, would I have told you that I am going to prepare a place for you? When everything is ready, I will come and get you, so that you will always be with me where I am" (John 14:2–3; NLT).

Fill your mind with what awaits a follower of Jesus when they depart from this life. That is what brought peace to Thomas Dorsey and prompted his plea for the Lord to take him home to heaven.

Charles Spurgeon preached, "Christian, meditate much on heaven. It will help thee to press on, and to forget the toil of the way. This vale of tears is but the pathway to the better country: this world of woe is but the steppingstone to a world of bliss."

In the context of chapter 14, Jesus is acknowledging that there will be times, especially at those occasions of death, when we will be troubled. We can replay those agonizing thoughts over and over in our minds and be imprisoned by despondency. We don't have to stay in that troubled state, however. We can replace those anguished thoughts with these truths:

1) Who I know—"You believe in God; believe also in me."

2) Where I will go—"I will come and get you so that you will always be with me where I am."

Say this out loud: "Who I know. Where I will go." No troubling storm in this life can take those truths from us. That is what we need to focus on when we are experiencing the heavy emotion of grief and the fear that accompanies death. One day we will go home to be with Jesus!

A Funeral or a Wedding?

We often hear the opening verses of John 14 at a funeral service. The assurance of a home in heaven is very comforting at those moments. The promise in the passage, however, becomes even more inspirational when we understand that Jesus is using wedding imagery and language from the wedding customs of his day.

In the traditions of a Jewish wedding, after the marriage covenant was sealed, the bridegroom would depart. He would go to his father's house and make preparations for his bride to come and live with him by adding an addition to the father's home. When the work was complete and the father gave permission, the son would return to get his bride. Hear John 14 through the grid of a Jewish wedding.

"I am going to prepare a place for you" (v2). That is a pronouncement from the groom. "When everything is ready, I will come and get you" (v3). That was Jewish wedding custom.

I wonder if the disciples didn't turn to one another and say, "His funeral announcement sure sounds like a wedding"?

In Jewish wedding custom, the groom would return with his wedding party. The shofar would be blown to signal that it was time for the wedding festivities to commence. Listen again to 1 Thessalonians 4.

> For the Lord himself will come down from heaven, with a loud command, with the voice of the archangel and with the trumpet call of God, and the dead in Christ will rise first. After that, we who are still alive and are left will be caught up together with them in the clouds to meet the Lord in the air.

And so we will be with the Lord forever
(1 Thessalonians 4:16-17).

In that passage, Jesus (the groom) is returning for the Church (his bride). The bride will go out to meet the groom to be escorted to the home prepared for her. Then the wedding celebration begins.

What is the first ceremony in the Bible?—It's the wedding of Adam and Eve. What is the last ceremony in the Bible?—It's a wedding! In an incredible narrative hook the end of the story is linked to the beginning of the story. In Genesis there is a wedding and the man and the woman are with God in Paradise until they are driven from his presence and from the Garden because of their disobedience. At the end of Revelation, Paradise lost becomes Paradise restored. Once again, we are in the presence of God, and there is a wedding celebration.

> "Let us rejoice and be glad and give the glory to Him, for the marriage of the Lamb has come and His bride has made herself ready." It was given to her to clothe herself in fine linen, bright

and clean; for the fine linen is the righteous acts of the saints.

Then he said to me, "Write, 'Blessed are those who are invited to the marriage supper of the Lamb.'" And he said to me, "These are true words of God" (Revelation 19:7–9; NASB).

What a glorious future awaits us! That longing inside us for home will one day be completely satisfied.

For we live by faith, not by sight. [*Faith in who we know and faith in where we will go.*] We are confident, I say, and would prefer to be away from the body and at *home* with the Lord (2 Corinthians 5:7–8; all emphasis added).

Adoniram Judson, a missionary in Burma for 40 years, captures the attitude we should possess when he writes, "I am not tired of my work, neither am I tired of the world; yet when Christ calls me Home, I shall go with the gladness of a boy bounding away from school."

That is a word picture that works for me. As a boy there was no more longed for time of day than for the school bell to ring. No one had to say, "You're dismissed." I was out of the school building almost as fast as a backrow Baptist is out the church's door on a Sunday morning. Like a boy bounding away from school, one day I will be away from this troubled world. I am going home.

In the mid-60s, Simon and Garfunkel were singing "Homeward Bound". The lyrics of the song spoke of the loneliness of life on the road and expressed their desire to be home. Our longing for home, however, flows from our soul's yearning cry to be home in heaven. The lyrics of a little-known Fanny Crosby hymn capture that cry. It is entitled, "Going Home Rejoicing".

> We are going home rejoicing,
> Where our Father's dwelling stands,
> We are going home rejoicing,
> To a house not made with hands;
> We are going home to Jesus,
> Who redeemed us with His blood,
> Hallelujah! hallelujah!
> Soon we'll cross the swelling flood.

Insight and Inspiration:

"Precious Lord, Take My Hand" was Martin Luther King's favorite song. He often invited gospel singer Mahalia Jackson to sing it at civil rights rallies. Dr. King's last words before his assassination were a request to have the song played at an event he was scheduled to attend that evening.

Don't simply read these words from the magnificent hymn "How Great Thou Art," sing like nobody is listening.

> When Christ shall come with shout of acclamation
> And take me home, what joy shall fill my heart!
> Then I shall bow in humble adoration
> And there proclaim: "My God, how great thou art!"
> Then sings my soul, my Savior God, to Thee,
> How great Thou art, how great Thou art.
> Then sings my soul, my Savior God, to Thee,
> How great Thou art, how great Thou art!

Surely your goodness and love will follow me all the days of my life, and I will dwell in the house of the Lord forever (Psalm 23:6).

Set your sights on the realities of heaven, where Christ sits in the place of honor at God's right hand. Think about the things of heaven, not the things of earth (Colossians 3:1b-2; NLT).

Chapter 10

Touring Heaven

A few years back a wave of books appeared that have been referred to as "heaven tourism" books. [26] They were stories about people who claimed they had near-death experiences and had gone to heaven before they were revived.

For example, Baptist minister Don Piper's book, *90 Minutes in Heaven*. In the storyline of the book, Don recounts how he was driving home from a conference when his car collided with a semitruck. Medical personnel said he died instantly and he was pronounced dead at the scene. For the next ninety minutes, Piper claims he experienced heaven where he was greeted by those who had influenced him

---

[26] Blogger Tim Challies labeled the genre "Heaven Tourism" and candidly dismissed one bestseller in the category as "pure junk, fiction in the guise of biography, paganism in the guise of Christianity."

spiritually during his life. He heard beautiful music and felt incredible peace. Piper, according to the book, miraculously came back to life and the bliss of heaven was replaced by a painful and grueling journey of recovery.

Then there is a book entitled *Heaven Is for Real*, also written by a pastor. Todd Burpo tells the story of his four-year-old son Colton who claimed he visited heaven while under anesthesia for an appendectomy. Colton described meeting his miscarried sister and his great-grandfather, who died before he was born. He also claimed he sat on Jesus's lap while the angels sang to him. He saw Mary standing beside Jesus's throne, and he met the Holy Spirit (who, according to Colton, is "kind of blue"). Colton also got a halo and real wings; and he saw Jesus on a rainbow-colored horse.

The bestselling Christian book for over a decade was *Heaven Is for Real*. It sold over ten million copies. *90 Minutes in Heaven* remained on the *New York Times* Bestseller List for five years and sold approximately seven million copies. Both books were also made into movies. Can you say, "Cha-ching"? There is money to be made in heaven tourism books. Their financial success prompted a flood of similar books to be written.

Question: Is it not a troubling indictment on the discernment skills of Christians that the best-selling book for over a decade was an implausible account of heaven spun from the imagination of a four-year-old boy? In my opinion, the answer is a resounding Yes!

John MacArthur confronted such heaven tourism accounts when he pointedly wrote:

> For anyone who truly believes the biblical record, it is impossible to resist the conclusion that these modern testimonies—with their relentless self-focus and the relatively scant attention they pay to the glory of God—are simply untrue. They are either figments of the human imagination (dreams, hallucinations, false memories, fantasies, and in the worst cases, deliberate lies),

or else they are products of demonic deception.[27]

Randy Alcorn, who has done extensive writing on the topic of heaven, would concur with that assessment. He wrote, "Satan labors to give people an inaccurate view of heaven...Some of his favorite lies concern heaven."[28]

Satan does have a vested interest in deceiving people about heaven. He wants to mislead us about our future home because so much comfort in the dying process and so much inspiration for living is found in an accurate understanding of heaven.

Heaven tourism books sell because people are fascinated with the topic of heaven and an afterlife, but those books have only added to the confusion and have compounded our misconceptions about heaven. A significant amount of that confusion could be removed by dispelling two of the most common misconceptions.

---

[27] MacArthur, John, "The Burpo-Malarkey Doctrine" (18 Oct., 2012), Quoted in a Review by Phil Johnson of Grace to You, accessed Oct. 20, 2012, http: //www.gty.org/Blog/B121018.

[28] Material in this chapter is adapted from Randy Alcorn's very helpful book, *Heaven* (Tyndale House Publishing, 2008).

Misconception #1: The Present Heaven Is Where We Will Live Forever

Paul wrote about being away from the body and at home with the Lord (2 Corinthians 5:8–9). At the moment of death our soul goes to be with the Lord in heaven and our body is laid to rest in the grave. We await Jesus's return. At that moment, the body is raised, transformed, and reunited with the soul that comes with Jesus at his second coming (1 Thessalonians 4). That is all review of earlier chapters.

John expounds further on what happens when Jesus returns. He gives us the most detailed exposition on heaven in the Bible.

> Then I saw "a new heaven and a new earth," for the first heaven and the first earth had passed away, and there was no longer any sea. I saw the Holy City, the new Jerusalem, coming down out of heaven from God, prepared as a bride beautifully dressed for her husband. And I heard a loud voice from the throne saying, "Look! God's dwelling place is now among the

people, and he will dwell with them.
They will be his people, and God him-
self will be with them and be their God
(Revelation 21:1–3).

The present heaven is a place of transition for the
soul between a believer's past life on earth and
the future resurrection life on the new earth. The
exact location of the present heaven is unknown,
but we're told the new heaven will be located on
the restored and perfected new earth.

In the creation account in Genesis, God created
the physical realm and called it good. He has never
given up on his original plan for human beings
to rule the earth for his glory. That is what Jesus
was referring to when he spoke of the "renewal of
all things."

"Truly I tell you, at the *renewal of all things*, when
the Son of Man sits on his glorious throne, you who
have followed me will also sit on twelve thrones"
(Matthew 19:28; all emphasis added).

Jesus used a fascinating Greek term when he spoke
of the "renewal of all things"; the word is *palingenesia.* It is a compound word derived from the words

palin meaning "again," and the word *genesia*, which means "beginning." *Palingenesia*—Genesis again!

Isaiah and other prophets spoke in detail about the earth being returned to the perfection of God's original creative work. Peter preached that Jesus would remain in heaven until the time came for the final restoration of everything (see Acts 3:20–21). Paul writes, "But with eager hope, the creation looks forward to the day when it will join God's children in glorious freedom from death and decay" (Romans 8:21–22; NLT).

Our eternal dwelling place will be the new earth, the restoration of creation as it was before the Fall. In another incredible narrative hook the consequences of sin's entrance into the world in Genesis 3 are all undone when the new heaven and the new earth appear. God's original plan for mankind is fulfilled and Paradise lost becomes Paradise regained.

That alone removes all the silly misconceptions of heaven being a place where we will sit on fluffy clouds, play harps, and chat with St. Peter at the Pearly Gates. But that very image of heaven has spawned another prevalent misconception, which is, heaven will be boring.

Misconception #2: Heaven Will Be Boring

If we are honest, we would admit that we have all wondered about this. Perhaps that thought entered your mind while singing the final verse of "Amazing Grace." "When we've been there ten thousand years...we've no less days to sing his praise than when we'd first begun." All together now, ten thousand more times. That doesn't sound appealing. The concept of an eternal church service doesn't exactly spin my top.

In Mark Twain's story of Huck Finn, Miss Watson, a rather stodgy old church lady, tells Huck about heaven. Huck later mused: "She said all a body would have to do there was to go around all day long with a harp and sing, forever and ever. So I didn't think much of it. But I never said so. I asked her if she reckoned Tom Sawyer would go there, and, she said, not by a considerable sight. I was glad about that, because I wanted him and me to be together."

Huck's words actually reflect Mark Twain's personal belief about heaven. He wrote on another occasion, "I'll take Heaven for the climate and Hell for the society."

The science fiction author Isaac Asimov wrote: "I don't believe in an afterlife, so I don't have to spend my whole life fearing hell, or fearing heaven even more. For whatever the tortures of hell, I think the boredom of heaven would be even worse."

In a Gary Larson "The Far Side" cartoon, he depicts a man in heaven sitting on a cloud wishing he had brought a magazine.

The all-too-prevalent misconception is that heaven is going to be one big bore. But from the glimpses of heaven given to us in the Bible, we know that heaven will be full of joy. The picture Jesus left us with is one of merriment, of music, dancing, and feasting. "Come and share your master's happiness!" (NIV), "Let's celebrate together!" (NLT), "enter into the joy of your master" (NASB); these are the words Jesus used in a parable to describe the rewards of heaven (Matthew 25:21,23). C.S. Lewis writes, "Joy is the serious business of Heaven."

Let's ponder a deep theological question prompted by the polka classic, "In Heaven There Is No Beer." Will there be beer in the new heaven and the new earth? I'm not trying to be irreverent or flippant with the question. I want to challenge your misconceptions of heaven.

Recall the description of the wedding supper that takes place in heaven:

"Let us *rejoice* and be *glad* and give him glory! For the wedding of the Lamb has come, and his bride has made herself ready" (Revelation 19:7; all emphasis added).

Isaiah writes of this wedding feast also:

"On this mountain the Lord Almighty will prepare a feast of rich food for all peoples, a banquet of aged wine—the best of meats and the finest of wines" (Isaiah 25:6).

Now a critique of the song lyrics: "In heaven there is no beer." We don't know that. Apparently, there is aged wine in heaven. What is not in heaven is evil. The sanctification and the glorification process are complete; we are sinless and pure. There is rejoicing and celebrating. I don't know, but there may be beer in heaven.

Benjamin Franklin said, "Beer is proof that God exists, and wants us to be happy." Again, I'm not trying to be irreverent or provocative. I simply want to challenge your concept of what heaven is like.

The song lyric continues: "That's why we drink it here. Right here." Reflect upon that lyric. Isn't it saying, "Heaven is going to be so boring that we better have fun here while we still can"? "If we're going to spend eternity in a mundane church service, we better drink up now"? That misconception is the lie of Satan.

The song concludes with this line, "And when we're gone from here, Our friends will be drinking all our beer!" Someday life will end for each one of us. Hopefully that reality will cause us to be more concerned with the eternal destination of our friends' souls than with whether or not there is beer in heaven.

Dr. David Jeremiah draws this conclusion, "It's safe to say we won't be bored in heaven. Heaven is going to be the most exciting, adventure-filled place your mind can imagine, multiplied by trillions."[29]

---

[29] What Will Heaven be Like? Dr. David Jeremiah, Turning Point, June 13, 2017.

Attempting to describe the glorious nature of our home in heaven, Paul wrote:

"No eye has seen, no ear has heard, and no mind has imagined what God has prepared for those who love him" (1 Corinthians 2:9; NLT).

The second misconception naturally raises our curiosity as to what we will do in heaven. Here is some of what we can look forward to:

1) Heaven will be a place of continuous learning, growth, and development. We will never exhaust exploring our Creator. God by nature is infinite and we will spend an eternity growing in our understanding of him. We will be able to visit face-to-face with our awesome God (Revelation 22:4).

2) We will serve God and one another (Revelation 22:3). Labor, however, will no longer be toilsome or a burden. It will be fulfilling and bring us pleasure and joy.

3) We will plant and build. The prophet Isaiah, speaking of the new earth, wrote, "They shall build houses and dwell in them; they will plant vineyards and eat their fruit" (Isaiah 65:21).

4) We will be reunited with loved ones who knew Jesus as their Savior. We will recognize one another in heaven.

5) We will make millions of new friends. We will get to interact with people from all periods of history.

6) We will never come to an end of exploring the Creator's handiwork. Creation will be our playground. C.S. Lewis pictured even the most beautiful and wondrous aspects of our present life on earth as "shadowlands" in comparison with the reality of our eternal home.

"Come, Lord Jesus"

The closing words in the great drama of redemption recorded in the Bible are these: Jesus says, "Yes, I am coming soon." To which John responds, "Amen. Come, Lord Jesus" (Revelation 22:20).

"Come, Lord Jesus" is the equivalent of the Aramaic expression "Maranatha." That became a term used as a salutation by the early Christians. They wouldn't say, "Goodbye," they would say "Maranatha." In other words, "Remember the Lord is coming. Be ready and encouraged by his return."

Living under the adverse conditions of Roman oppression, a believer's morale was lifted by the hope of the return of Jesus and a future in heaven. That is our hope too.

"Come, Lord Jesus."

Inspiration and Insight:

When John Owen, the great Puritan preacher, lay on his deathbed, his secretary wrote to a friend in his name, "I am still in the land of the living." Owen saw it and said, "Change that and say, 'I am yet in the land of the dying, but I hope soon to be in the land of the living.'"

> "Heaven is not just a destination; Heaven is a motivation."
> —Warren Wiersbe

> "...understanding our destination shapes all we do in preparing for a trip, and it especially determines our enthusiasm to take the trip."
> —Amy Harwell, *Ready to Live, Prepared to Die*

When Ronald Reagan was running for governor of California, a woman confronted him one day and berated him severely. She said, "I wouldn't vote for you if you were St. Peter."

Reagan smiled and replied, "No problem. If I were St. Peter, you wouldn't be living in my district."

> "We may be surprised at the people we find in heaven. God has a soft spot for sinners. His standards are quite low."
> —Desmond Tutu

> "Good people don't go to heaven; forgiven sinners do."
> —Andy Stanley

Chapter 11

I Can't Leave You with a Bad Goodbye

S aying goodbye has been the subject matter of some of the most heartrending and thought-provoking songs ever written. The title of this chapter, for example, is found in the lyrics of the stirring Clint Black duet with Wynonna Judd, "A Bad Goodbye." That song title and the lyrics within the song beg the question: Is there a good goodbye? Especially when leaving refers to the severing of a relationship by death, can there be a good goodbye?

The answer is that there is at least a better goodbye. People who have prepared to die have given careful consideration to how they will say goodbye to those they leave behind.

Some choose to diminish the pain of the inevitable goodbyes in life by never really saying hello. They reason that it would make more sense not to get too attached because the closer you get, the more it's going to hurt when the moment of goodbye comes. As a result, their relationships are distant and emotionally shallow. A person grieving the death of someone they truly love, however, never wishes they had not known the deceased. They regret that the relationship wasn't deeper and that it didn't last longer. They consider the anguish of bereavement well worth it. As Garth Brook sings in "The Dance", we could miss the emotional pain of life, but then we would miss the dance.

Others choose to avoid the pain of goodbye by playing a damaging game of pretense and denial of death's approach. But when they do, they are left with a bad goodbye. Harriet Beecher Stowe reminds us, "The bitterest tears shed over graves are for words left unsaid and deeds left undone."

The remorse-filled remark I frequently hear from clients processing their grief is that they never got to say goodbye. When a last goodbye is a bad goodbye, or if goodbye was never expressed, it compounds grief for those left behind. In Gestalt psychology this is referred to as *unfinished business*. It is a term that a therapist would use to describe the emotions surrounding past experiences that have been avoided or repressed. When feelings are not fully processed because they are too overwhelming or traumatic, they are left unresolved and they linger. They are then carried into our present life where they interfere with our ability to be emotionally present. The unfinished business that is left from bad goodbyes complicates and prolongs the grieving process.

Cause of Death

We have all heard the overused joke from Will Rogers—"When I die, I want to die like my grandfather who died peacefully in his sleep. Not screaming like all the passengers in his car."

But seriously, if you could choose, what would you prefer to be the cause of your death? What would you like the coroner to write on your death certificate for cause of death? A coroner has never written "Death by chocolate" even though that would definitely be my first choice.

The cause of death that I would dread the most would be Alzheimer's disease. The protracted period from diagnosis to death from Alzheimer's disease has been called "the long goodbye" and for good reason. As the disease slowly progresses, the distinctive features of an individual's personality fade away along with his or her cognitive skills and ability to remember. Friends and family of an individual with Alzheimer's disease become strangers, and, in a sense, the individual with Alzheimer's becomes a stranger to family and friends. It is a long goodbye and a dreadfully bad goodbye.

John Wyatt in his book *Dying Well* shares this thought-provoking observation:

> If you ask people how they would like to die, most people today will say: "I want to die in my bed while I am asleep. I don't want any warning, any premonition, any awareness. I just want to go suddenly, like a light." Yet the strange thing is that, if you were to go back four hundred years and ask people the same question, they would generally agree that sudden, unexpected death was the worst possible

way to die. To be catapulted into eternity with no chance to say goodbye, no chance to ask for forgiveness or to ensure your loved ones were provided for, no chance to prepare yourself to meet your Maker—what a terrible way to die.[30]

"No chance to say goodbye...what a terrible way to die."

In Mitch Albom's book *Tuesdays with Morrie*, the main character Morrie Schwartz is dying of ALS. Morrie makes this insightful and inspiring statement, "It's horrible to watch my body slowly wilt away to nothing. But it's also wonderful because of all the time I get to say goodbye."[31]

The Gift of a Good Goodbye

As you prepare to die, resolve to leave your loved ones the gift of a good goodbye. Too often people wait until they are too emotional, too ill, or too physically exhausted and then it's too late. Too often people leave unfinished business because

---

[30] John Wyatt, *Dying Well*, (London, InterVarsity Press, 2018) p. xvi.

[31] Mitch Albom, *Tuesdays with Morrie*, (New York: Doubleday, 1997), p. 50.

they have avoided the uncomfortable conversations about dying, even their own impending death.

The Conversation Project is a national collaborative effort to support end-of-life discussions. It was started by a group of media, clergy, and medical professionals dedicated to helping people discuss their wishes for end-of-life care. According to the Conversation Project, 90 percent of Americans know they should have a conversation about what they want at the end of life, yet only 26 percent have done so.[32]

In order to leave your loved ones the gift of a good goodbye you need to discuss all the practical matters surrounding the end of life. When you arrive at conclusions in these matters it is important to make a paper trail. Put your funeral preferences in writing, draw up a will, prepare Medical Directives, and determine who will serve as Power of Attorney and Medical Power of Attorney.

The benefits of such planning include reduced family conflict because you have provided clear instruction for them when difficult decisions must be made. This will also help your loved ones

---

[32] For helpful information see theconversationproject.org.

experience a healthier bereavement without guilt or fear that they have failed to honor your wishes.

The gift of a good goodbye also means you have addressed with the significant people in your life the unfinished relational business you may have dragged with you—the unforgiveness, the resentments, and the unreconciled relationships. Express to those you love how much they have meant to you in life. Talk about your shared memories and talk about what you hope for their future.

Theologian Charles Hodge wrote, "It is important that when we come to die, that we have nothing to do but die."

Such an intriguing phrase—"nothing to do but die." No unfinished business.

Grief Recovery and Saying Goodbye

After death arrives, those left behind need the closure of saying a final goodbye. When I assist people in that task through the funeral process, I will sometimes use the lyrics from a Carrie Underwood song entitled "Starts with Goodbye." The song lyrics acknowledge the sadness that comes with goodbye, but the lyrics also insist that moving on with the rest of your life may require it.[33]

We want to push back against that reality because we mistakenly think that letting go and moving on is forgetting how important someone was, still is, and always will be. The deeper and more authentically we love, the more pain we feel when a loved one is no longer with us.

One reason why many get stuck in the grieving process is that the emotions attached to the loss, although painful and draining, are all that remain of the person who is gone. Holding on to grief seems to keep that connection alive. Sometimes we need and want the pain because it's a memorial to the love that was there. In some ways not wanting to let go is a beautiful thing, but it leaves you mired in your anguish, and your loved one would not want you to remain there.

My favorite philosopher, which is Winnie the Pooh, said this, "How lucky I am to have something that makes saying goodbye so hard."

---

[33] "Starts with Goodbye" appears on Carrie Underwood's 2005 album *Some Hearts*. Written by Hillary Lindsey and Angelo Petraglia.

There is a lot of wisdom in Pooh's words. "How lucky I am to have something (or someone) that makes saying goodbye so hard." Goodbyes are always hard. With love there is always a corresponding measure of sadness that comes with loss. In fact, one of the paradoxes in the experience of grief is that the most wonderful memories from the past suddenly become the most painful reminders in the present. Those memories remind us of what we've lost. But with time those wonderful memories of the past are reframed as reminders of the love that was there. We can be grateful for the sadness we feel in that regard; it is evidence of the love that was there.

Grief recovery begins with a good goodbye. During a funeral benediction, I have found it helpful to remind people of the origin of the word goodbye. Goodbye is a contraction of the phrase "God be with thee." It's English in origin, a parting farewell in the true sense of that word, "May you fare well. May God be with thee."

Goodbye was originally a parting blessing. One person would say "God be with thee," as their friend departed. That chap may have responded in return, "Yes, God be." Then over a period of time, "God be" evolved into our expression "goodbye." Perhaps that occurred because the British speak as if they have a mouthful of marbles. In giving the gift of a good goodbye we pronounce God's blessing on our loved one.

Until We Meet Again

Leaving the gift of a good goodbye also includes giving your loved ones assurance of your beliefs regarding salvation, your confidence that you are going to heaven, and your hope for reunion one day with them. That hope is captured in the German phrase "Auf Wiedersehen," which doesn't mean goodbye in our understanding of the word. It is closer in meaning to "Until we meet again," or "Until I see you again." It's a hopeful affirmation of reunion that proclaims that someday we will be together again.

In the Christian faith that hope is built upon the promise of Jesus, who said, "I am the resurrection and the life. He who believes in me will live, even though he dies."

It took a while to get there, but let's reflect for a moment on the most hope-filled and astounding statement ever uttered throughout time. It is found in verse 25 of John chapter 11.

A bit of context to set the scene: A significant number of people have gathered to mourn and grieve with Martha and Mary because their brother Lazarus has died. Lazarus has been in the tomb for four days. We could go to Bethany even today and see a cave that is identified as Lazarus's tomb. So amazing is the event that is about to unfold that one generation after another generation throughout history have pointed to the place that Lazarus lay dead and retold the story of what happened.

We know how this story ends, but in that moment, no one there knew. People are wailing. There is intense mourning. Verse 35 says that even Jesus wept. In a tender moment we are given the privilege to glimpse the heart of God. Jesus wept.

By way of contrast, the Greeks described their gods by one word, *apatheia.* That word has carried into our language and we derive our word "apathetic" from it. An interesting word, it is from the root word *pathos*, a term which means "suffering" or "emotion." Add an "a" or an alpha privative and it means to have "no feeling" (*a + pathos*). The Greek gods were *apatheia.* That meant they had no ability to empathize.

Empathy is another interesting word, from *en* (in) + *pathos* (emotion/feeling). Empathy is the capacity to understand or feel what another person is experiencing. It is the capacity to place oneself in another's place. The gods that the Greeks worshipped did not have that ability. They were *apatheia,* but our Savior weeps with us and for us. That is so far removed from some people's concept of God as being uninvolved and unconcerned or even unaware of the emotional pain in their lives.

Jesus wept because this is not the way it was meant to be. He wept because he walked into a situation where enemy number one, death, was reigning. He wept and he was deeply moved in spirit and troubled (v33). He then asked for the stone to be rolled away from the entrance of the tomb, and he called out in a loud voice, "Lazarus, come out!" The dead man came out, his body was wrapped with strips of linen, and he had a cloth around his face (v43–44).

And then...and then the curtain falls. We don't know anything more about what happened. We are given no further information. What?

We don't know anything about the shock and surprise that must have overtaken the stunned mourners. We don't know anything about the tearful reunion of Mary and Martha hugging their brother. We don't know anything about the conversations that Lazarus had after that. You can imagine the questions, "Lazarus, what was it like?" Imagine the celebration that must have taken place. But we know nothing of that because we are not told.

Tradition says Lazarus lived another 30 years. Maybe that's true. We don't know. In fact, the last mention of Lazarus in the Bible is in the next chapter of John.

"So the chief priests made plans to kill Lazarus as well [*i.e., as well as kill Jesus*], for on account of him many of the Jews were going over to Jesus and believing in him" (John 12:10–11; all emphasis added).

Why are we not given further information about Lazarus? Because that was not John's purpose in writing his account of the Good News. He wrote to challenge us to respond to the question Jesus asked after his incredible claim:

"I am the resurrection and the life. The one who believes in me will live, even though they die; and whoever lives by believing in me will never die. Do you believe this?" (John 11:25-26)

That is the most important question ever asked in history. "Do you believe this?" Your eternal destiny rests upon your answer to that question. Your ability to leave your loved ones with a good goodbye also depends upon your answer.

Do you believe this?

Inspiration and Insight:

"We'll Never Say Goodbye" — written in 1889 by Anzentia Chapman after the death of her daughter Eva

> Our friends on earth we meet
> with pleasure,
> While swift the moments fly,
> Yet ever comes the tho't of sadness,
> That we must say goodbye.
> We'll never say goodbye in heav'n,
> We'll never say goodbye,
> For in that land of joy and song

We'll never say goodbye.

How joyful is the tho't that lingers,
When loved ones cross death's sea,
That when our labors here are ended,
With them we'll ever be.
We'll never say goodbye in heav'n,
We'll never say goodbye,
For in that land of joy and song
We'll never say goodbye.

"The pain of leaving does not compare
with the joy of being reunited."
                    —Charles Dickens.

Chapter 12

Last Words

T he final words spoke by an actor or actress as they die in a movie scene can be a pivotal and enduring moment in the film. Take for example a movie that is said to have changed cinema forever, the 1941 classic *Citizen Kane*.

The film opens with one of the most enigmatic and talked-about death scenes in film history as media magnate Charles Foster Kane (Orson Welles) lies on his deathbed and utters a single final word, "Rosebud." That word frames the movie's narrative as a reporter then tries to uncover its significance. At the end of the movie we discover that "Rosebud" referred to a sled from Kane's childhood, and that provides insight into understanding his tragic life.

Mel Gibson played the role of William Wallace in the movie *Braveheart.* Wallace, the legendary Scottish patriot, unified the clans of Scotland and won battles against the English before being captured, tortured, and executed. He was offered a quick death if he would utter the word "mercy." Wallace instead shouts his inspiring final word, "Freedom!"

Tom Hanks's dying words in *Saving Private Ryan* helped him secure an Academy Award nomination for Best Actor. Hanks, playing the role of Captain Miller, is fatally wounded on a mission to rescue Private Ryan (Matt Damon). Captain Miller's last words to Private Ryan were, "Earn this. Earn it." Earn the life he has been given by the sacrifice made by Miller and his men. It's a deeply touching moment that shaped Ryan's life as evidenced by the movie's final scene; an elderly Ryan asks his wife if he has lived a life worthy of the sacrifices made for him.

There is a fascination with the last words of the dying. Perhaps final words are of interest to us because we think they might offer a glimpse into the afterlife. Maybe we will hear a final piece of wisdom, words of forgiveness, or longed-for assurance of love. The expectation that last words will provide insight or inspiration, however, are more frequently fulfilled in movies with stirring soundtracks than in real life. But occasionally throughout history some final words have been faith affirming and noteworthy of future generations.

President George Washington's dying words, for example, were, "Doctor, I am dying, but I am not afraid to die." He then folded his hands over his chest and according to his wife Martha said, "It is well."

The dying words of others stand as testimonies of humankind's defiance toward God. Actress Joan Crawford was filled with anger when her maids began to pray at her death bed and her last words were, "Don't you dare ask God to help me." (Not a good way to exit from the stage of life.)

The most significant and the most studied final words throughout history are the seven statements from Jesus as he hung upon the cross. Entire books are devoted to the exposition of these seven statements. In this chapter, we will take a brief devotional look at the insight and guidance each of these statements provides in our aim to die well.

Luke records this concise statement to set the scene:

"When they came to the place called the Skull, they crucified him there, along with the criminals—one on his right, the other on his left" (Luke 23:33).

According to Roman historians, it was common for those who were being crucified to utter blasphemies and curses toward those who were involved in the gruesome execution. Cicero noted that the executioners would sometimes even cut off the tongues of the criminals so that the soldiers would not have to listen to their vile vindictiveness. But as the darkness of the human heart was displayed in all of its ugly cruelness, Jesus uttered words filled with grace. The first of his seven final statements was:

> *"Father, forgive them, for they do not know what they are doing"* (Luke 23:34).

Dr. Ira Byock, an international leader in palliative care, teaches four simple phrases that carry the core wisdom of what people who are dying have taught him about what matters most in life. He outlines those statements in his book *The Four Things That Matter Most*. The phrases are: Please forgive me, I forgive you, Thank you, and I love you.[34]

---

[34] Ira Byock, *The Four Things That Matter Most- A Book about Living,* (Atria Books—Simon and Schuster, 2004).

The readiness to apologize for our failures and a readiness to grant forgiveness to those who have sinned against us is essential to dying well. The cycles of grievances and grudges, bitterness and retaliation that have marked life complicate the dying process. In order to live and to die well and at peace with God, we cannot be nursing resentments or bearing a burden of guilt. Forgiveness can remove that acrimony and resentment. Forgiveness can carry the weight of guilt away.

One reason to forgive, is not what it does for the offender, but what it does for you as the forgiving party. As someone said, "Letting go of a rattlesnake might help the snake, but it benefits you as well."

The emotional work of forgiveness, however, is more difficult than sermons often make it appear. The key to forgiving others is to understand how undeserving we are to be forgiven by God. When we forgive others, we bear witness to the grace and forgiveness that we ourselves have received.

Shortly before his death, Martin Luther wrote these words, "We are beggars; this is true." We are spiritually bankrupt and could never merit the great price paid for our forgiveness, the precious blood of

Jesus (see 1 Peter 1:18–19). Fortunately, God never said, "Earn this. Earn it!" Forgiveness is offered freely and is possible only because Jesus paid the debt for our sin on the cross.

The forgiving response of Jesus was so extraordinary that one of the criminals crucified next to Jesus had a remarkable moment of awakening. Luke records this criminal's words directed first to the other criminal, "We are punished justly, for we are getting what our deeds deserve. But this man has done nothing wrong." Then Luke records his request directed to Jesus, "Remember me when you come into your kingdom." His request was neither eloquent or theologically profound. Yet, he is a powerful example of an authentic deathbed conversion.

Jesus's response to him was immediate, *"Truly I tell you, today you will be with me in paradise"* (Luke 23:43).

Jesus had remained silent in front of his accusers during the sham trials, he had ignored the insults of the crowd and the scorn of the first thief, but he responded immediately to this cry of faith. What we learn from this dramatic moment is that no one is beyond the reach of God's grace. The thief was a violent man and more than likely a murderer, but there is no sin that God's grace cannot pardon. A hymn writer inspired by that truth, penned the words, "the vilest offender who truly believes, that moment from Jesus a pardon receives."[35]

The thief didn't do anything to merit the gift of salvation. In fact, he couldn't do anything to earn it. He could not walk in paths of righteousness because there was a nail through his feet. He could not perform good deeds because there were nails through both hands. The way of salvation is wonderfully simple. It is never earned or deserved.

The second statement of Jesus brought such comfort and hope to the early Christian community that they frequently chose to have the thief's words, "Jesus, remember me," inscribed as an epitaph on their gravestones. They recognized that all humanity chooses to identify with either the rebellious thief or the repentant thief.

The third statement: *"Dear woman, here is your son,"..."Here is your mother"* (John 19:26–27).

---

[35] *To God be the Glory*, lyrics by Fanny Crosby.

The words are full of tenderness and thoughtfulness; a dying son makes what provision he can for his mother's care and protection. As the eldest son, Jesus carried a responsibility for his widowed mother. Now, hours before his death, he hands that responsibility to the person he trusted the most. And his words were not ignored. John adds a concise note, "from that hour the disciple took her into his own home."

Dying well includes addressing the practical needs of loved ones we leave behind. The reassurance that those needs are met help a dying person let go.

As we examine the Gospel accounts we learn that darkness now settled over the scene. With the darkness came an unsettling silence as each onlooker tried to process the significance of the disappearance of the sun. Apart from the moans coming from the crosses, little was heard by those witnessing the gory spectacle. Then, out of the blackness, came an agonizing fourth cry: *"My God, my God, why have you forsaken me?"* (Matthew 27:46).

Behind this painful cry is the theological truth of 2 Corinthians 5:21—For God made Christ, who never sinned, to be the offering for our sin, so that we could be made right with God through Christ. (NLT)

The sins of the world were laid upon Jesus. Sin brings separation from God. Jesus was experiencing that break in fellowship with the Father when he uttered the forth statement. His words were taken from the first verse of Psalm 22, a well-known Messianic psalm. The priests would often read this psalm before the Passover lamb was sacrificed. So with the fourth statement, Jesus was conveying to us, "I am the Passover Lamb for your sin."

The famous artist Rembrandt was commissioned by Frederik Hendrik, Prince of Orange, to paint a series of five paintings based on the last events of Jesus's life. His second work in that series is entitled "Raising of the Cross." It is now located in a museum in Münich. The painting portrays Jesus nailed to the cross as soldiers lift it to an upright position.

Rembrandt placed himself in this painting twice, two self-portraits. The most obvious is seen in the figure of a man wearing a blue artist's beret who is assisting in raising the cross. Rembrandt created a visual metaphor. By placing himself in the painting, he acknowledged that he was a sinner and that it was his sins that took Jesus to the cross.

A second self-portrait also appears in the painting. This time in the form of an overseer of the crucifixion, a man who looks directly at anyone viewing the painting. His fixed gaze perhaps questioning, "Don't you see that your sin led Jesus to the cross also?"

The lyrics in an old spiritual inquire, "Were you there when they crucified my Lord?" The imagery intensifies with each verse, and the repeating questions place everyone on the witness stand. "Were you there when they nailed him to the cross? Were you there when they pierced him in the side? Were you there when the sun refused to shine? Were you there when they laid him in the tomb?" Our answer to those questions should cause us to tremble, tremble, tremble because Jesus did endure the cross for your and my sin.

After the fourth statement, it seems that the final three statements from the cross came in rapid succession.

"Later, knowing that everything had now been finished, and so that Scripture would be fulfilled, Jesus said, *'I am thirsty'*" (John 19:28).

Max Lucado in his book *He Chose the Nails* questions why in his final moments Jesus was committed to fulfilling prophecy. Lucado concludes, "He knew we would doubt. He knew we would question. And since he did not want our heads to keep his love from our hearts, he used his final moments to offer proof that he was the Messiah."[36]

Fulfilled prophecy is just one line of evidence that provides reassurance that Jesus is who he claimed to be. Some scholars list 322 Old Testament prophecies that describe the Messiah. Prophecies written hundreds of years before Jesus's birth foretell specifics of his life. Jesus fulfilled every one of those prophecies. That reassurance provides security and strengthens our faith as we contemplate passing from this life.

The sixth statement: *"It is finished!"* (John 19:30)

---

[36] Max Lucado, *He Chose the Nails*, (WORD PUBLISHING, Nashville, 2000).

This statement is not the lament of a victim but the shout of a victor. It wasn't the whimper of a defeated man; it was a triumphant cry of completion. By his death, Jesus completed in full the work of redemption necessary for our salvation. He accomplished everything he came to do.

In the Greek text this statement is a single word—*tetelestai*. The root of the word is *telos*, meaning "the end." Archaeologists have repeatedly found its Latin equivalent scrawled across tax receipts used in those days. In this context it means "paid in full." Jesus completed his work in saving us; he paid our debt. Not just part of the debt, not just a down payment that we now need to continue making installment payments on. Our debt is canceled, paid in full.

"He forgave us *all* our sins, having canceled the charge of our legal indebtedness, which stood against us and condemned us; he has taken it away, *nailing it to the cross*" (Colossians 2:13-14; all emphasis added).

> Oh the bliss of this glorious thought
> My sin, not in part, but the whole
> Is nailed to the cross and I bear
> it no more.

It is well, it is well with my soul!

George Washington's last words and the inspiration for the lyrics in Horatio Spafford's marvelous hymn "It is Well," flow from the glorious truth of the sixth statement, "It is finished!" Our salvation is secure and, therefore, we can die in complete assurance of everlasting life in heaven.

Jesus's last words were, *"Father, into your hands I commit my spirit."* When he had said this, he breathed his last (Luke 23:46).

"Father, into *your hands*..."; not into the grave or into the dark unknown, but into the loving *hands* of God. God's arms are open and his hands extended to embrace his dying children.

"Father, into your hands *I commit* my spirit." The word commit means to place in safekeeping and to entrust. Dying well involves an act of relinquishment, releasing oneself into God's hands.

The expression, "Let go and let God" takes on its deepest application in the process of dying. There is a kind of tug of war between holding on and letting go in dying. Sometimes people need permission to let go. They need to hear an assuring word that their loved ones will be cared for, that loved ones are waiting on the other side, and that someday we will meet again.

The final statement by Jesus was so transforming that it has been taken up by his followers as a model to follow. Stephen, as he was being stoned to death, prayed, "Lord Jesus, receive my spirit" (Acts 7:59).

When Charles Lindbergh discovered he had terminal cancer he wrote down the following words to be read at his graveside service:

> We commit the body of Charles A. Lindbergh to its final resting place; but his spirit we commit to Almighty God, knowing that death is but a new adventure in existence and remembering how Jesus said upon the cross, "Father, into thy hands I commend my spirit."[37]

The final statement of Jesus is drawn from the closing line of an evening prayer recited by devout Jews. At the close of the day, as they were about

---

[37] Benjamin P. Browne, *Illustrations for Preaching* (Nashville, TN: Broadman Press, 1977), p. 85.

to slip off into sleep, these words from Psalm 31 were included in their prayer: "Into your hands I commit my spirit; deliver me, Lord, my faithful God" (Psalm 31:5).

Begin to make those words a part of your evening prayer. Pause to consider as you do that you are one day closer to "a new adventure in existence."

Inspiration and Insight:

A doctor and family friend to Thomas Edison noticed that the great inventor was trying to say something during his final moments of life. He leaned close to Edison's bed and heard him whisper, "It's very beautiful over there." Those were his last words.

When Harriet Tubman died in 1913, she gathered her family around and they sang together. Her final words were, "Swing low, sweet chariot."

It is written that Beethoven, nearing death, said, "I shall hear in Heaven."

D.L. Moody reportedly turned to his boys who were at his bedside and said, "If God be your partner, make your plans large."

On his deathbed, John Wesley fervently spoke his last words. He said the same thing twice: "The best of all is God is with us. The best of all is God is with us."

William Carey, the missionary to India, said, "When I am gone, speak less of Dr. Carey and more of Dr. Carey's Savior."

> "Jesus, remember me when you come into your kingdom."
> —An unnamed dying thief that we will meet in heaven

Chapter 13

This Changes Everything

The phrase, "This changes everything," became trendy when Steve Jobs promoted the iPhone with that tag line. There have been discoveries or inventions or events down through the pages of history that have dramatically altered the world and changed how we live. The iPhone is just one example. Here are a few more:

The discovery that the Earth was round and that one would not fall off the edge by sailing past the horizon. That changed everything!

Gutenberg's invention of the printing press in 1439. That changed everything! (By the way, the driving force behind his effort was his desire to print and mass produce the Bible.)

In 1879, Thomas Edison perfected an invention that many had worked on and the light bulb illuminated the darkness. That changed everything!

On the sandy beaches of Kitty Hawk, North Carolina, in 1903, the Wright brothers made their historic 12-second, 120-foot flight in a powered flying machine. That changed everything!

But we need to pause to gain perspective. The single most earthshaking and transformative event throughout history is not on that list. The event that dramatically changed everything is the resurrection of Jesus from the dead!

The resurrection validated Jesus's astounding claims to be God, the only source of forgiveness for sin, and the only avenue for eternal life. The comfort and hope that a Christian has at death is based upon Jesus's resurrection. His resurrection is the proof and the pledge of our resurrection. In our pluralistic culture, those claims are rejected as being exclusive and narrow-minded. Yet those claims cannot be dismissed or ignored because of that one event in history that changed everything.

That was Paul's line of reasoning when he wrote:

And if Christ has not been raised, then all our preaching is useless, and your faith is useless. And we apostles would all be lying about God—for we have said that God raised Christ from the grave. But that can't be true if there is no resurrection of the dead. And if there is no resurrection of the dead, then Christ has not been raised. And if Christ has not been raised, then your faith is useless and you are still guilty of your sins. In that case, all who have died believing in Christ are lost! And if our hope in Christ is only for this life, we are more to be pitied than anyone in the world (1 Corinthians 15:14–19; NLT).

One Distinguishing Difference

There are four major world religions today that were started by or founded upon a single person. Those four religions are Buddhism, Judaism, Islam, and Christianity. These four religions all have highly influential leaders who have changed the history of the world.

Buddhism was founded by Siddhartha Gautama, (aka the Buddha—"the enlightened or the awakened one"). After vowing to find truth, he achieved enlightenment through meditation, and the principles of Buddhism were formulated.

Judaism was founded upon Abraham (aka father Abraham). He was the man God selected to be the father of a chosen people, the Hebrew race. A promised Messiah would emerge from Abraham's lineage.

Islam was started by Muhammad, though most Muslims would not word it that way. Muhammad claimed that he received a revelation from God that called all people to submission to Allah.

The Christian faith is founded upon Jesus. God took on human flesh and then gave his life as a payment for sin to provide an avenue through which people could be reconciled with their Creator and live with him forever.

Each of these men share a common trait that when compared reveals a major difference that cannot be ignored. They all died. When religious leaders die, their grave sites are often enshrined. It becomes more than a grave site; it now becomes a place of historic religious importance. Elaborate structures are created in order to honor the burial place of that religious figure.

The Buddha's body was cremated, and the relics were placed in monuments or stupas. For example, the Temple of the Tooth in Sri Lanka is the place where the right tooth relic of Buddha is supposedly kept. Thousands of people come from all over the world to visit this site.

Abraham's tomb, located in Hebron, is called the Cave of the Patriarchs. It is a massive structure built over the caves where Abraham's body was buried along with Isaac, Jacob, Sarah, Rebecca, and Leah. They are considered the patriarchs and matriarchs of the Jewish faith.

Mohammad's tomb is known as the Mosque of the Prophet. It is undoubtedly the largest and most elaborate tomb ever constructed.

Then we come to Jesus. But in his case, we can only speculate where the tomb is that Jesus was buried. There is a site known as the Garden Tomb, but no one can say with certainty that it is where Jesus's body was placed. So why doesn't Jesus have an enormous and enshrined tomb like the other religious founders? Because his body is not there! His tomb is empty! He rose from the dead!

Josh McDowell was asked, "Why can't you refute Christianity? In response, he said,

> For a very simple reason, I'm unable to explain away an event in history—the resurrection of Jesus Christ. After more than 700 hours of studying this subject and thoroughly investigating its foundation, I came to the conclusion that the resurrection of Jesus Christ is either one of the most wicked, vicious, heartless hoaxes ever foisted upon people, or it is the most important fact of history. The resurrection issue takes the question "Is Christianity valid?" out of the realm of philosophy and makes it a question of history.[38]

The evidence for the resurrection is compelling and incontrovertible. In 1998, Lee Strobel, a reporter for the *Chicago Tribune* and a graduate of Yale Law

---

[38] Josh McDowell, *More Than a Carpenter*, (Carol Stream, IL Tyndale Momentum, 2009), p. 125.

School, published *The Case for Christ: A Journalist's Personal Investigation of the Evidence for Jesus.* Strobel had been an atheist, but he was compelled by his wife's conversion to Christ to attempt to refute the key Christian claims about Jesus. In his efforts to do so he found the evidence was so compelling that he also became a Jesus follower. He concluded that it was "the most rational and logical step" he could possibly take.[39]

One Question

In a very insightful and instructive scene from Jesus's life, John records one of the most pertinent and pressing questions of life. At this point, Jesus was near the pinnacle of his popularity. Large crowds followed him because they saw the miracles he had performed. In truth, many in the crowd followed Jesus because they saw him as their meal ticket. Jesus had just miraculously fed a massive crowd with only five loaves and two fish. They wanted him to continue to provide for them like Moses provided manna during the exodus from Egypt.

---

[39] Lee Strobel, *The Case for Christ: A Journalist's Personal Investigation of the Evidence for Jesus,* (Grand Rapids, MI. Zondervan, 1998).

Jesus tells the crowd, "I have not come to bring bread. I have come to be bread. I am the bread of life. He who comes to me will never go hungry, and he who believes in me will never be thirsty" (my paraphrase of John 6).

The crowd was concerned about the emptiness in their stomachs, but Jesus spoke of a deeper hunger. He spoke about a spiritual hunger, about the emptiness in their souls. When we are physically hungry, our bodies have ways of signaling that we need sustenance. Our stomach will rumble audibly, and food will smell especially appetizing. We are so in tune with the needs of our body that we recognize these signals easily, but we are far less familiar with the signs that our soul is hungry.

When our soul is hungry, we sense an emptiness, a void, a nagging longing for something more in life. We then chase empty solutions that never feed the soul—sex, shopping, status, more stuff, alcohol, or some diversion, but nothing satisfies for very long. Just as there is physical food that can best be described as junk food, there is also spiritual food that can be described as junk food. We need to nourish the soul with what satisfies and that is the Bread of Life.

One of the words for life in the Greek language is the word *bios*, and it means physical life, material life. We get our word biology from this word. There is another Greek word for life and it is the word *zoe*. It is life that transcends the physical, it is eternal life. When the crowds were coming to Jesus looking for bread, he said:

"I am the bread of life [*zoe*]. Whoever *comes* to me will never be hungry again. Whoever *believes* in me will never be thirsty" (John 6:35; all emphasis added).

He is saying, "You have a hunger that transcends your physical hunger. You have a thirst that transcends your physical thirst. You have a *zoe* need that you are attempting to fill with a *bios* solution, and that will fail you." Jesus is trying to expose their need. He says, "Guys, you are concerned with your stomach, and I am concerned with your soul."

Snickers candy bars has a very effective ad campaign. Their tag lines are "Only Snickers satisfies" and "You're not you when you're hungry." There are great spiritual parallels to those Snickers ads. What you eat to feed your soul transforms you. Jesus alone is the food that truly satisfies soul hunger.

Notice the words "comes" and "believes" in verse 35. They are invitation words, a call to place your faith in Jesus as your Savior. Jesus extends the invitation to come throughout John's Gospel. "Come and see...come and follow...come and be with me." Coming to Jesus involves making a choice.

The call to believe is also found throughout John's Gospel. In fact, John explains that it is the reason his Gospel was written:

"Jesus performed many other signs in the presence of his disciples, which are not recorded in this book. But these are written that you may *believe* that Jesus is the Messiah, the Son of God, and that by *believing* you may have *life* in his name" (John 20:30–31; all emphasis added).

How did the crowd in chapter 6 respond to the invitation? The crowd displayed an obstinate misunderstanding.

On hearing it, many of his disciples said, "This is a hard teaching. Who can accept it?"...From this time many of his disciples turned back and no longer followed him (John 6:60,66).

One more quick Greek lesson: "This is a *hard* teaching." The Greek word for hard is *scleros.* We speak of arterial sclerosis—a hardening of the arteries. There is a spiritual hardening of the heart that takes place in chapter 6. Many of those in the crowd turned away and no longer followed Jesus. At this point Jesus turned to the twelve and asked, "You do not want to leave too, do you?"

"Lord," answered Simon Peter, "*Who else* should we go to? Your words have the ring of eternal life! And we believe and are convinced that you are the holy one of God" (John 6:68–69, Phillips, all emphasis added).

In his response, Peter presents us with life's most pertinent and pressing question: "Who else?" Who else could we turn to if we seek eternal life? Who else made the claim to be God? Who else rose from the grave proving they were God?...Not the Buddha, not Abraham, and not Mohammad! Those dudes are still in the grave!

Do you want to build your life and base your hope for eternity on the words of dead men or upon the One who came back to life? The resurrection proves that what Jesus claimed is true and it exposes all other religions for what they are—just the schemes and speculations of mere mortals who stepped onto the stage of history for a season. "The most rational and logical step" is to place your faith in Jesus and accept his offer for eternal life.

Two Epitaphs

The consequence of your choice is captured in the epitaphs on two contrasting tombstones. One of them marks the resting place of Mel Blanc—the man of a thousand voices, the famous voice of countless characters in *Looney Tunes* cartoons. In accordance with his instructions, his family had his signature phrase, the words that ended so many cartoons, engraved upon his memorial stone: "That's all, folks."

If that epitaph summarizes Blanc's view of death, then it is truly tragic. "That's all, folks" expresses all the hope that a secular person has when death arrives. When life is over, the candle is blown out, there is nothing more, that's all there is.

By contrast, the epitaph on Frank Sinatra's tombstone reads: "The best is yet to come." For the follower of Jesus, indeed the best is yet to come. That confidence rests upon the empty tomb and the resurrection of Jesus from the dead.

What is your decision regarding Jesus and his claims upon your life? Your decision to receive Jesus as your Savior will change everything. It is the key to living with purpose and dying in peace.

Inspiration and Insight:

> When a person of considerable accomplishment dies, the people giving eulogies are likely to mention how much the world has been impoverished by that person's death. They might say, "Humanity has suffered a great loss. A bright light has gone out in the world. The world will certainly miss their many talents." We cannot speak this way about Jesus's death. The truth is the world was not impoverished by Jesus's death; it was enriched. Jesus's death and resurrection forever altered the meaning of death.
>
> —(Source unknown)

"If Jesus rose from the dead, then you have to accept all that he said; if he didn't rise from the dead, then why worry about any of what he said? The issue on which everything hangs is not whether or not you like his teaching but whether or not he rose from the dead."
—Tim Keller

"One Day"—John Wilbur Chapman (verse 4 and refrain)
One day the grave could conceal him no longer,
One day the stone rolled away from the door;
Then he arose, over death he had conquered;
Now is ascended, my Lord evermore!
Living, he loved me; dying, he saved me;
Buried, he carried my sins far away;
Rising, he justified freely, forever.
One day he's coming—O, glorious day!

"Do not be afraid. I am the First and the Last. I am the Living One; I was dead, and now look, I am alive for ever and ever! And I hold the keys of death and Hades."

—Jesus's words recorded in Revelation 1:17-18